For Willy, Carlos, Junior and Ramon

Prologue

Perhaps one of the saddest episodes in the New Testament is the moment when Jesus, betrayed and arrested, turned to look at Peter after hearing him say, for the third time, "I do not know him." Luke writes, "And the Lord turned and looked at Peter; and Peter remembered the word of the Lord, how he had said to him, 'Before the cock crows today, you will deny me three times.' " What follows must recall the most sorrowful hour of Peter's life: "He went out and began to weep bitterly" (Luke 22:61–62).

"I do not know him." How could Peter ever forget that denial? And he repeated it, twice. For the rest of his life, Peter must have remembered those words many a time, and whenever they rang in his ears, the tears and sorrow of that night would have descended upon him again. What is it like, we should ask ourselves, to betray the friend we most loved and then to have that person die the next day? What is it like, we might wonder, to carry such grief to our grave, with never a chance for reconciliation, never again a morning when we could make up? All the counseling and therapy in the world, all the mental effort at remembering our last time together and trying to force on it a different outcome, all the imagined embraces and apologies, would not erase the pain in that memory. Visualizing the dead Jesus hanging on the cross, Peter must have endured grief such as this. Perhaps the closest most of us might come to such an experience would be our losing a friend or a child, a husband or a wife, a sister or a brother, and realizing how much more love and care we could have given to a person who will now never return to us.

It does not do to say that since Jesus had told the disciples he would rise three days after his death, therefore their grief would not have been too shattering. *We* know how the story turns out, but they did not understand what he meant when he said, "The Son of Man is to be handed over to men and they will kill him, and three days after his death he will rise" (Mark 9:31). They lived through those hours of Jesus' suffering and death without knowing the outcome. The disciples had to endure the loss and the bitter memory of their own cowardice without any foreknowledge of a happy ending to make their sorrow easier to bear. Perhaps if we had been disciples, curiosity alone might have led us to post ourselves near the tomb of Jesus to watch what a resurrection would look like, presuming, of course, that we had the least bit of comprehension of what Jesus meant when he said he would rise "on the third day." But the disciples did not do this, which suggests that they were not anticipating Jesus to return. The gospel tells us that Peter went out and wept bitterly. Was he thinking that he would never again be able to walk up to Jesus the next morning, maybe searching for a welcome, maybe impulsively throwing his arms around him and saying (how much he must have wanted to do this!), "I'm sorry"? Pain like that would never be erased.

Peter and Jesus must have had a stormy relationship at times. I can imagine their arguing, on some occasions perhaps fiercely, about the direction of Jesus' mission, and Jesus telling Peter, "Not *that* way, *this* way!" "Get behind me, Satan!" would hardly have been an appropriate response to a small misunderstanding. Jesus almost screams at Peter, "You are not thinking as God does, but as human beings do" (Mark 8:33). At stake was a fundamental difference about the meaning of discipleship, about the nature of the kingdom, about power and weakness, about success and failure. This difference would have remained a sore point between them. Peter could not quite see why Jesus had to go to Jerusalem, why he had to keep talking about dying, why he would surrender to his enemies without a fight. And still, at the Last Supper, Peter would insist, "Even though all should have their faith shaken, mine will not be" (Mark 14:29), and "Lord, I am prepared to go to prison and to die with you" (Luke 22:33).

Would it be too farfetched to imagine Jesus replying, "Never disown me? Peter, you and the others have failed to understand me from the start! All along the way your eyes and ears have been closed. I talked about suffering and you were thinking about rewards. On the road to Jerusalem, I predicted the cross and you started dreaming about crowns. You welcomed the rich when they wanted to see me and you shoved the blind, the unclean, and the children away. You did not trust me when I was asleep on the boat, you resented the crowds that followed us and guarded your wallets because you were afraid that you would have to feed them, you became insecure when those who didn't walk with us were casting out demons in my name, you are intimidated by those in positions of authority and so you want power yourself. Never disown me? Peter, before the night is over, you will have said you do not know me three times over." And Peter shot back, "Even though I should have to die with you, I will not deny you." But Jesus knew Peter, and he knew that down deep Peter, for all his affection, had not yet grasped that his teaching and his way were what God wanted. Was Peter cowardly and impulsive? Perhaps. But it may be closer to the mark to find here two very close friends, one of whom had not yet fully understood the other. And now with Jesus dead, there was no chance for Peter to pour out his heart, to say yes, that he loved Jesus, that he still did not see why Jesus had to die, but that given one more chance he would not have let his fear, his confusion, his deep-seated misgivings get the better of him. Given another chance, he would have died beside his friend.

An imaginative reconstruction like this may help us to sense the extraordinary feeling behind the questions Jesus addressed to Peter after the resurrection. For what Peter had thought impossible now actually happened. Jesus was there, standing in front of him, and asking, "Simon, son of John, do you love me more than these?" (John 21:15). The echo of Peter's "though all may have their faith in you shaken" is drowned by Jesus' "do you love me more than these?" And with Jesus' asking three times "Do you love me?", Peter can finally answer what he had been anguishing to be able to say to him, "Lord, you know everything; you know that I love you." His pledge at the supper, "Even though I should have to die with you . . .," is taken up by Jesus: "When you grow old, you will stretch out your hands, and someone else will dress you and lead you where you do not want to go" (John 21:18). Eventually Peter does lay down his life; eventually, he dies with Jesus.

I open this book on the baptismal promises with these scenes from the gospels involving Jesus and Peter because, like Peter, we have already professed our loyalty to Jesus. In accepting baptism we too promised to follow Jesus. We joined our lives to his. And yet, our discipleship can likewise be a stormy one. Our following also has its tender points, its moments of doubt, of misunderstanding, of forgetting, of being more impressed with human affairs and values than with the things of God. Being a disciple of Jesus entails a life-long growth in freedom, in knowledge of Jesus, and in knowledge of ourselves. Weaknesses are uncovered, temptations have to be faced, forgiveness has to be sought. We have much to learn about faith and the kingdom of God. It may even happen that, like some of Jesus' early listeners, we find his teaching to be too much for us and, without actually leaving the Church, we have inwardly distanced ourselves from him. Our living, in effect, announces to others, "I do not know this man about whom you are talking" (Mark 14:71). Perhaps we have not accepted Jesus' teaching about forgiveness, or about wealth, or about the necessity of taking up our cross, or about serving others, or about welcoming the stranger. Perhaps we live more by cash or by compromise than we do by faith. Perhaps we are more concerned with how we appear before others than how we stand before God. Perhaps we are timid in our practice of the faith, easily threatened when large numbers of people do not share our values, or disturbed when the bishops speak out on issues such as nuclear arms or the economy. Perhaps we are somewhat embarrassed by the gospel's remembering Jesus as a friend of tax collectors and prostitutes, or as an evangelist might record today, a friend of drug addicts, unwed mothers, and people with AIDS.

But we have an advantage over Peter and the other disciples, because we can read about how Jesus returned to rebuild their faith and restore their confidence in his love and friendship. Jesus has not died on us. Our relationship with Jesus never needs to end on the note of rejection, of fear, of doubt, or of betrayal. Perhaps we have not taken the kingdom of God all that seriously. Perhaps some human relationship has momentarily blinded us to the values for which Jesus stands. Perhaps for a while we lost interest in Jesus because he appeared a little too human and familiar, and we went looking for exotic forms of religious experience. Maybe we have been scandalized by the behavior of other Christians, or maybe we were never really convinced that we could not serve both God and money. For all of the gospel's talk about following Jesus, we may have been more impressed by people who have power, or business connections, or social prestige, or physical strength. Or perhaps, like the disciples themselves, we deserted Jesus and what he stands for, and we do not know how to find our way back. Whatever the case, our Jesus, the Jesus of the Church's faith, stands in front of us and asks in a tone that each of us must hear for ourselves, "Do you love me?" This, as I see it, may be the primary benefit of renewing our baptismal promises. We need to say yes once again to him, to the real Jesus around whom we can throw our arms and say, like Peter, "Lord, you know all things; you know that I love you." And we must also hear him say to us, "Follow me."

WHY WE RENEW THE PROMISES
The renewal of the baptismal promises occurs in the context of the Easter Vigil service. The Church's ancient custom was to receive people fully into the community during the Easter Vigil, when they would be baptized, sealed with the Spirit, and receive the Eucharist for the first time. For us, the Holy Saturday liturgy provides an opportunity to recall our own baptism, and provided that we have taken the Lenten season seriously as a time for spiritual renewal, renewing our baptismal commitment can be a truly graced moment. Promises should not be taken lightly, especially promises made to God. We made, and now renew, those promises because we desire to let our lives be grounded in and guided by the gospel. Promises look toward the future. They do not cancel out the possibility of failure, of going back on our word, of temporarily losing sight of the direction of our lives. Yet failure should never stop the follower of Jesus from trying to be faithful, or from starting over, any more than the fear of failure should

6

cripple the heart's desire to give itself, totally and unreservedly, to another.

Why make promises? We make promises because we want to do something about the shape of our lives. We want to entrust ourselves to others and to face the future with hope. At a time when many men and women seem less willing to make and keep commitments, the followers of Jesus need to resist the temptation to become sceptical about the possibility of making lifelong promises and remaining faithful to them. Promises, after all, give expression to our desires: what we want to do, what we want to become, what we want to give, how much we want to love. To lose confidence in the possibility of making and keeping promises is to jeopardize the human heart itself, which is the seat of all our desiring. Besides, desires which are truly lifegiving ultimately trace their origin to the Spirit of God. To dismiss the possibility that human beings can make and keep promises, and their human obligation to do so, is to lose faith in the Spirit which prompts us to do and to dare great things with our lives.

There is, however, another reason why the church includes in the Easter Vigil the renewal of the baptismal promises together with the profession of faith, and that reason is catechetical. *Catechesis* means instruction. Literally, it comes from a Greek word which means "to make hear" or "to echo thoroughly." Something becomes familiar and well-known to us because we have heard it over and over. The promises, of course, are quite familiar: Do you renounce Satan? and all his works? and all his empty promises? So too the profession of faith: Do you believe in God, the Father almighty, creator of heaven and earth? Year after year we listen to these questions at the Easter Vigil, and again, provided we have taken the time to think about them, they can reenforce the whole structure of our faith. For most of us, the Church's liturgy is the place where our ongoing catechesis takes place. But precisely because the questions are so familiar, they can also sound like unimaginative religious formulas which stir neither our minds nor our hearts. If we reflect on those questions ahead of time, however, then those ancient phrases can ring again with the faith of the Church as they have done through the ages. Rather than sounding like tired, uninteresting questions, the words of the baptismal promises and profession of faith will focus our attention once more on the ground and direction of our lives.

Nevertheless, the fact seems to be that the promises, at least for most people, do not mean a great deal. "Do you renounce Satan?" Well, of course we do! But what does that mean? Who in his or her right mind would not renounce Satan, and his works, and his empty promises? Perhaps the formulation functions as a symbol; perhaps we owe it to our sacramental tradition to retrieve its significance. If so, then we should do whatever we can to help one another understand fully and unambiguously exactly what we promised at our baptism, and what we are recommitting ourselves to each year when the Church invites us to renew those promises. The question which John Paul II addressed to the Catholics of France on his visit there could apply to all of us. The pope had asked, "France, eldest daughter of the Church, are you being faithful to the promises of your baptism?"[1] Likewise, speaking to each of us personally, the Church could rightfully inquire: "You who have allowed yourself to be called Christian, are you being faithful to what you pledged when you accepted baptism?"

THE DECISION TO BE AND TO REMAIN CHRISTIAN
The sacrament of baptism really serves as the foundation for Christian living. We cannot improve upon the promises made there to follow Christ, for in consenting

to die and rise with Jesus we surrendered our lives to the holy mystery of God. In letting ourselves be washed with the water of baptism and anointed with oil in the sign of the cross, we promised to be followers of Jesus, for life. We chose to be identified as Christian. Some people wish they had been older when they received baptism so that they could have made a conscious choice for Christ, and others reach the conclusion that by being baptized as children they were unfairly obliged to follow the Christian way. Both groups may believe that they were deprived of the chance to be catechumens, to explore the church and its teachings, and to come to a mature decision about whether or not to follow Jesus.

These are difficult problems and I cannot hope to treat them fully here. Yet at least I can make a few brief observations. No one, of course, *has* to be a Christian; the decision to follow Jesus must always be a free one. If someone chooses not to be Christian, we have to respect that decision, without attributing bad will. This might prove quite painful for us, especially if the person is a family member or a close friend. Obviously, some individuals simply never take Christian faith seriously in the first place, while others lose the little faith they had. Some seed always falls on rocky ground (Matthew 13:20). The bottom line, however, is that we are made for freedom, and in matters of religious belief, as in everything else, the rights and the freedom of individuals must be respected.

It is worth adding that Christian wisdom has long grasped the truth that human beings become free only by obeying God. This insight into the dialectical relationship between freedom and law lies at the heart of St. Paul's theology and the religious belief of the Old Testament. The Book of Deuteronomy referred to the two ways, the way of life and the way of death (Deuteronomy 30:11–20): freedom and life will come to the

9

people only if they observe the law of the covenant. Of course, one must obey the living and true God, and not some idol or false representation of the divine mystery. To follow a false god is to become enslaved and dehumanized. The same thing holds true for Christians. We become free and fully human only as we remain faithful to Jesus. But it must be the real Jesus, and not a fabrication of him tailored to our limited notions of what he ought to be like. Some people prefer a Jesus who never challenges their loyalties or never calls the status quo into question; their capacity for self-knowledge is never stretched. Really to lead people to Jesus, therefore, is to lead them to freedom. "Where the Spirit of the Lord is," Paul writes, "there is freedom" (2 Corinthians 3:17). That is why being Catholic always involves more than laws, practices, and precepts. These things can lead people to freedom, but only if they genuinely express the mind and heart of the gospel. Otherwise, they may even dehumanize people if they impose burdens which God never intended us to carry (Acts 15:10). Nevertheless, people who turn away from the Church because they cannot be bothered with its laws and practices may in fact be turning their backs on the road to genuine freedom and fully human living. But like the prodigal son, this may be a lesson we have to learn through the experience of loss, powerlessness, shame, confusion, and remorse.[2]

To return to our point, then, the fact remains that every time we take the Eucharistic bread into our hands and raise the Eucharistic cup to our lips we ratify the promises which our parents and godparents spoke in our name. We may have been unconscious then of what was happening to us, but that is no longer the case if as mature believers we have continued to celebrate the Eucharistic liturgy. We are saying, in effect, that we are throwing in our lot with Christ. What he stands for, we stand for. What he loves, we love. His way of life, his example and teaching, will become the pattern for our own.

In receiving the Eucharist, we are asking the Father to keep tracing the Christ-sign—the sign of the Cross—over our lives; and this sign was first traced over us when we were initiated into the dying and rising of Jesus. The vows pronounced by couples at their wedding, or those taken by men and women on their entry into a religious community, may specify the direction of the baptismal commitment. But those vows do not improve upon that initial promise to be a disciple of Jesus, totally and unreservedly. If a Catholic Christian wishes to renounce belonging to Christ, then she or he simply has to reject the Church's faith in the sacrament of the Lord's body and blood.

Most of us were baptized as children, and therefore it may not be until we become parents or godparents ourselves that we have an opportunity to appreciate the symbolism and religious meaning of the sacrament. Baptized children are, of course, fully members of the Church. It should be no surprise that parents want to have their children brought into the Church, even though the children cannot speak for themselves. We are not consulted, after all, about the families into which we are born, or about the civil society which will become our cultural heritage. It makes perfect sense to be born also into the family of believers, for faith is a treasure and knowing Jesus is God's gift. Christian parents will naturally want to hand on to their children their knowledge of God and their experience of faith.

The sacrament of baptism is the sacramentality of Christian existence itself. The ritual can be celebrated in a matter of minutes, but the sacrament requires a lifetime to unfold. In a way, our families and our Christian community are always baptizing us into the mystery of

Christ, always leading us further along the way of discipleship. During this process, our religious sensibilities mature, we learn what Christian living means, and we have many occasions in which to own our baptism formally and publicly: at the Easter Vigil service, in the sacrament of confirmation, certainly, but principally in the celebration of the Eucharist.

WHAT ARE WE COMMITTING OURSELVES TO?

As I mentioned, the formula of the promises may be so familiar to us that we no longer appreciate the radical nature of the words and the weight of the commitment which we are undertaking. One way to make this clear is to frame the promises in a way that highlights their significance and suggests some points we might reflect upon during the Lenten season by way of preparation for the Easter Vigil. Consider questions like these:

Do you accept Jesus as your teacher, as the example whom you will strive to imitate and as the one in whom the mystery of God's love for the world has been fully revealed?

The formulation may sound new, but the belief implied in the question is ancient. It is simply asking, "Do you believe in Jesus Christ?"

Do you dedicate yourself to seeking the kingdom of God and God's justice, to praying daily, to meditating on the gospels and to celebrating the Eucharist faithfully and devoutly?

After all, Jesus told us to seek the kingdom of God before all else (Matthew 6:33), and he set us the example of human prayerfulness and intimacy with God. Thus, there can be no Christian life without prayer, and the Eucharist is its center. How can we recommit ourselves to the practice of our faith and not review the manner and frequency of our prayer, and the fidelity and reverence with which we celebrate the Lord's Supper?

Do you commit yourself to that simplicity of living which Jesus enjoined on his disciples? Do you commit yourself to resisting the spirit of materialism and consumerism which is so strong in our culture?

This puts some teeth into the ancient promise about renouncing Satan and his works. Needless to say, many other things could be included here. There are many forms of injustice, of greed, or of lording it over others; there are many ways to escape the penetrating light of God's truth. As the bishops of the United States wrote in their pastoral letter on the economy, "Christian faith and the norms of justice impose distinct limits on what we consume and how we view material goods."[3] From time to time, the Church needs to specify what has to be renounced, given the times and circumstances in which we live.

Do you accept responsibility for building community, for being people of compassion and reconciliation, for being mindful of those who are poor and oppressed, and for truly forgiving those who have offended you?

If being church means belonging to the Lord together, then what merit is there to believing in the "holy Catholic Church" unless we are ready to act as if we genuinely belonged to one another? How else would we live out this truth? To believe in the Church, the Holy Spirit, the communion of saints, and the forgiveness of sins calls for sincere dedication to promoting peace, justice, and reconciliation in whatever ways are open to us.

Will you try to thank and praise God by your works and by your actions, in times of prosperity as well as in moments of suffering, giving loyal witness to the risen Jesus by your faith, by your hope, and by the manner of your living?

The whole of a Christian's life is an act of worship, a daily living out of the basic desire to be with and for the God who has come close to us in Jesus. The whole of Christian existence must be a sign that God's reign in human hearts is a present reality; the kingdom of God is already in our midst, if men and women would only open themselves to it.

Do you surrender your lives to God as disciples and companions of Jesus? Do you believe that God is Lord of history, sovereign over nations and peoples, and that God's promise to redeem all of creation from its bondage to death and decay will one day be accomplished?

This is just another way of asking whether we have resurrection faith. The God whom we know in Jesus is the one who brings the dead to life, whose creative purpose cannot be frustrated even by sin and death. The God who is Father of our Lord Jesus Christ is the one who will raise our mortal bodies to be like Christ's. If Jesus really lives, then what logical choice do we have except to follow him? If Jesus has been raised, then the future of the world is tied to the power of God to bring the dead—all who have been God's faithful servants—into redeemed life.

It might be a good idea for us individually or as parish communities to develop a set of questions like these and to take one a week during Lent to think over and pray about. This is one way by which we can unpack the significance or the symbolic value of the liturgical formula for the promises we renew at the Easter Vigil.

THE PLAN OF THE BOOK

If we listen to the baptismal examination carefully, we should notice that there are two sets of questions with their corresponding promises. First, there is the renunciation of sin. The other side of this, of course, is the commitment to a renewed following of Christ. And secondly, there is a trinitarian profession of faith. We are asked whether we believe in the Father who creates us, the Jesus who redeems us, and the Spirit who animates the Church by drawing us into communion. The present tense of these verbs—creates, redeems, animates—is important, because the holy mystery of God remains ever active in our personal lives, in our communities, and in our world.

The first set of questions appears to be concerned with Christian practice: we refuse to let our living be subverted by the power of evil. The second set seems to be concerned with Christian beliefs: we assent to the doctrine about creation, about Jesus, about the forgiveness of sins, bodily resurrection, and eternal life. It could be argued that the two sets are inwardly connected, for practice and belief belong together. It is not a matter of practice first and then belief, or belief first and then practice. What we believe and profess—the doctrines to which we give the assent of faith—imply practice. Our Christian practice, that is, the way we live as men and women who have promised to follow Jesus, leads us to grasp Christian truth. We know the truth by doing it; or, to put the matter a little differently, we come to understand Jesus by following his teaching and example. Following leads to knowledge, and knowledge issues in love.

While Christian baptism provides the thematic background for this book, my intention here is not to discuss the history and theology of sacramental practice. We shall not be concerned with theological issues about whether baptism is necessary for salvation, or the nature of original sin, or why the teaching about limbo has disappeared, justifiably, from the Church's religious instruction. Rather, this is a book about what we are accepting when we commit ourselves to living in the company of Jesus. It is something one might read in preparation for the renewal of his or her baptismal promises at the Easter Vigil service, or if one is preparing to be the sponsor of a child or an adult at baptism. My aim is simply to help a person reflect upon, and grasp more firmly, the significance of what we pledge when we ratify our baptism. If our baptismal promises do not serve to make us more human, freer, more available to others, more capable of love and affection; if they do not enlarge our capacity for life and for wholehearted trust in God, then our baptism will have done us little good. Which is to say, if following Jesus does not serve to make us more human, then in a real sense Jesus has not been our savior. He will not have taken our sinfulness away. He will not have been the one whose love for us and whose faithfulness have been truly liberating and lifegiving.

This is also a book about Christian sacramentality in the broad sense. Whenever those who profess to be following Jesus witness to their faith by the integrity of their living and the uncluttered simplicity of their desire for God, then the sacrament of baptism is unfolding. The liturgy of the sacrament provides a window onto Christian existence, and it is through the lives of Christians, animated by the Holy Spirit, that Jesus becomes really present in our world.

Some readers may recall that the catechism used to distinguish three kinds of baptism: baptism of water, baptism of blood, and baptism of desire. The water baptism was the sacrament in the ordinary sense. Those men and women who were seeking full incorporation into the Church but who suffered martyrdom before they could be baptized by water were recognized as Christians because they had been baptized in their own blood. And baptism of desire embraced those men and women of good will who never had an opportunity to hear the gospel and respond to it, but would certainly have accepted Christ if God's will had been made known to them. The notion of baptism of desire harbored an insight, because the heart's desire provides the key for understanding the religious dimension of human experience. We could make the case that water baptism is basically the physicalization—or, more properly, the sacramentalizing—of our desire to follow Christ, for without that desire what would be the advantage of being baptized? What would baptism express? Without questioning the permanent validity of the sacrament, I would suggest that the desire to be with Jesus is what keeps our baptism alive.

Liturgical symbolism and ritual, like the baptismal promises themselves, remain empty and lifeless unless informed by faith. So too Christian existence would be drained of any religious meaning or credibility if it did not breathe with the desire for God. This desire, and the hope which springs from it, enriches and ties together every aspect of our lives. It shapes the way we understand ourselves and the world. Whether we are aware of it or not, the desire for God that we carry in our hearts can irradiate everything about us: our thoughts, our words, our actions, our values and decisions, our politics, the manner of our living—what we own, what we use, what we share,—our loyalties, our friendships, how we love, how we celebrate, how we deal with our mistakes, and how we die. Just as Jesus, God's word made flesh, is the flesh-and-blood sign of the presence of God, so are his followers the living signs of the reality of God's kingdom in the world. Just as Jesus sacramentalized the loving closeness of God, so too do the disciples of Jesus. The same Spirit which led Jesus to call God "*Abba*, Father" has been poured into our hearts, as St. Paul told the Christians in Rome (Romans 5:5). The life of the Christian unfolds as an outward sign of invisible grace.

As I indicated, the profession of faith which we make as we renew out baptismal promises consists of two parts. First, there is the renunciation of sin. The questions which the Church here puts to us concern what we do (or rather, what we must not do, if we wish to follow Jesus), and this is the material of the opening chapter. Secondly, there is the recommitment to Christian belief as the Church invites us to confirm our faith in the central Christian truths. The profession of faith has a trinitarian form, which thus provides a convenient format for the next three chapters. Wherever appropriate, I have remarked briefly on the gospel readings for the Sundays of Lent. Reading and meditating upon those texts in the context of the baptismal promises should enhance our participation in the Holy Saturday liturgy. The main purpose of the pages which follow is to encourage adult reflection on the meaning of the baptismal promises and their expression of Christian experience.

What are some of the elements of that experience? For now, it will be enough simply to list them, since they have been woven into the chapters which follow. They are (1) the experience of being created; (2) the experience of sinfulness; (3) the experience of forgiveness; (4) the experience of dying and rising with Jesus; (5) the experience of church; and (6) experiencing ourselves as people who desire and look for God. It seems to me that the profession of faith presupposes experiences such as these; otherwise, how would we really know what we are assenting to? For example, without such experiences, what would it mean to believe in God as the creator, or in Jesus who was crucified, died, and was raised? What would it mean to believe in the Church and the communion of saints, or in the forgiveness of sins? Is life everlasting simply a piece of information about what happens after death, or can we point to any present experience which confirms that a qualitatively different life has already begun, the life of which Jesus spoke when he said, "Now this is eternal life, that they should know you, the only true God, and the one whom you sent, Jesus Christ" (John 17:3)?

To know God the way Jesus knew God is to discover the depth and richness which comes from constantly living in the divine presence. And this possibility is ours, which is why we say, "I believe in the Holy Spirit." We come to understand the Christian experience by walking the Christian way, and we know the way is true because by walking it we feel ourselves deeply and joyously alive. Is this not the significance of Jesus' words, "I am the way and the truth and the life" (John 14:6)? Walking this way is like being born again and discovering for the very first time what human life can be. This, of course, is what being baptized into Christ Jesus is all about.

NOTES

1. As quoted by Eric O. Hanson, *The Catholic Church in World Politics* (Princeton, N.J.: Princeton University Press, 1987), p. 19.

2. In its "Instruction on Infant Baptism," the Vatican's Congregation for the Doctrine of the Faith commented: "Some people also object that baptizing infants is a restriction of their freedom. They say that it is contrary to the dignity of the children as persons to impose on them future obligations that they may perhaps later be led to reject . . . Such an attitude is simply an illusion: There is no such thing as pure human freedom, immune from being influenced in any way. Even on the natural level, parents make choices for their child that are essential for its life and for its orientation toward true values. A so-called neutral attitude on the part of the family with regard to the child's religious life would in fact be a negative choice that would deprive the child of an essential good. Above all, those who claim that the sacrament of baptism compromises a child's freedom forget that every individual, baptized or not, is, as a creature, bound by indefeasible duties to God . . ." The full text appears in *Origins* 10:30 (1981), p. 474–480.

3. *Economic Justice for All: Pastoral Letter on Catholic Social Teaching and the U.S. Economy* (Washington, D.C.: United States Catholic Conference, 1986), #75.

Chapter One

Do You Reject Satan?

When you were asked: "Do you renounce the devil and his works?"—what did you reply? "I do renounce." "Do you renounce the world and its pleasures?"—what did you reply? "I do renounce." Be mindful of your words, and never let the sequence of your bond be broken.

You are anointed as an athlete of Christ, as if to contend in the contest of this world.   St. Ambrose[1]

The gospel reading for the First Sunday of Lent is about the temptation of Jesus in the wilderness (Matthew 4:1–11, Mark 1:12–15, Luke 4:1–13), and this episode in Jesus' life is a suitable place for us to begin reflecting on what it means to reject Satan. In learning how to "reject Satan," we have Jesus as our example, as he withstood the temptations of Satan in the wilderness.

The story of Jesus in the desert immediately follows the account of his baptism by John in the Jordan. This sequence of events—baptism and then temptation—is not without significance for us, for it implies that there is a particular kind of struggle or testing which begins after the Spirit has been given. Jesus is baptized, the Spirit descends upon him, and then he is "led by the Spirit" (in the accounts of Matthew and Luke) into the wilderness to be tempted. Mark's version is stronger: the Spirit literally forced or shoved Jesus into the desert. Might the same pattern hold true for us? It is not at all uncommon for people to think that struggling with evil inclinations ends with conversion, and to some degree that is the case. But perhaps a different kind of struggle begins when a person comes to know Jesus and attempts to live according to his teaching and example. First we are baptized, and then our inner struggle begins, as the Spirit "leads" and sometimes "forces" us; for the life of Christ has started to grow within us and to displace the old self. We may feel like we have been shoved into a wrestling match with demons.

Christian existence appears to be marked by its own characteristic tension and temptation. All human beings experience temptation, but perhaps there is a kind of temptation which we undergo precisely because we are trying to follow Jesus and let our lives be guided by his Spirit. This is a possibility we need to explore. First, however, we must note the difference between Jesus' baptism and ours, because it bears upon the difference between the kind of temptation Jesus faced in the desert and the kind of temptation which we encounter as his disciples.

JESUS' BAPTISM AND OURS

Jesus' baptism stands as a preface to his public life; it signals the enthusiastic beginning of his ministry of teaching and healing. There, by the Jordan, the Spirit descended upon him and, as Matthew tells the story, a voice from heaven declared, presumably to those standing around, "This is my beloved Son, with whom I am well pleased" (3:17). Or, as Mark and Luke tell it, the voice is directed to Jesus, a voice which perhaps he alone can hear: "You are my beloved Son; with you I am well pleased" (Mark 1:11, Luke 3:22). Jesus received the baptism of John, the baptism of repentance. By accepting baptism at John's hands, Jesus demonstrated his oneness with all those who, prompted by John's preaching, were trying to set their eyes and hearts on the kingdom of God. He stood squarely with the politically oppressed people of Israel in their great hope that God would finally and definitively champion their longing for justice and righteousness. At this important moment in Jesus' life he is anointed with the Spirit to be the herald of God's kingdom. Here his messianic mission begins, and the temptation story which follows only underscores the connection between his baptism and his future ministry. Because of its association with his struggle in the wilderness, Jesus' baptism might well anticipate another struggle and another baptism, namely, his suffering and death (see Mark 10:38–39 and Luke 12:50).[2]

We, however, do not receive John's baptism, with all that it represented for the religious hopes of Israel. Rather, we are baptized—claimed (Romans 8:29–30), reborn (John 3:5), sealed (Ephesians 1:13), consecrated (1 Peter 2:9)—into Christ Jesus. "Or are you unaware," Paul wrote, "that we who were baptized into Christ Jesus were baptized into his death? We were indeed buried with him through baptism into death, so that, just as Christ was raised from the dead by the glory of the Father, we too might live in newness of life" (Romans 6:3–4). To be baptized is to be drawn into the mystery of the dying and rising of Jesus.

THE TEMPTATION OF JESUS IN THE DESERT

Just as there is a difference between Jesus' baptism and ours, so too there is a difference between the nature of his temptation and the temptations we experience. Three of the gospel writers report that after Jesus was baptized in the Jordan River by John, he was led into the wilderness to be tempted by the devil. Mark's account is the briefest: "At once the Spirit drove him out into the desert, and he remained in the desert for forty days, tempted by Satan. He was among wild beasts, and the angels ministered to him" (Mark 1:12–13). A number of motifs may be at work here. Jesus, like Adam, and therefore like all human beings, undergoes temptation. The garden of Eden was the place in which God placed Adam, and there Adam "named" the various beasts of the earth (Genesis 2:19), which is a way of saying that Adam was not only in charge of the animals; they also posed no threat to him. Instead of the lushness of the primeval garden, however, Mark draws on the image of the barren wilderness as a more fitting place in which to find the Son of God struggling against the powers of darkness. Yet even there, Jesus is in charge, and the wild beasts cannot harm him. Even in the wilderness, there are angels; even in the lonely and arid wastes of the desert, God's ministering spirits can be present. As a non-biblical Jewish writing puts it, "If you do good, my children, both men and angels shall bless you, and the devil shall flee from you and the wild beasts shall fear you and the Lord shall love you."[3]

By mentioning forty days, Mark seems to be recalling the people of Israel's long wandering in the desert after God had delivered them from Egypt. There they struggled with the mystery of the God who had loved them above all nations; they resisted that mystery of love and mercy, as the psalmist remembered:

"Oh, that today you would hear his voice: 'Harden not your hearts as at Meribah, as in the day of Massah in the desert, where your fathers tempted me; they tested me though they had seen my works. Forty years I loathed that generation, and I said: They are a people of erring heart, and they know not my ways. Therefore, I swore in my anger: They shall not enter into my rest' " (*Psalm 95:8–11*).

But Jesus does not test God in the desert. He trusts God, and therefore he will not ask God for signs. Throughout his life, Jesus would offer no resistance to the holy mystery which had claimed him. "The angels attended him" may be another way of stating that Jesus always remained one with the voice which had declared: "You are my beloved Son; with you I am well pleased" (Mark 1:11).

Jesus' encounter with Satan is deadly serious business. It was believed that the final age of the world would be marked by a cataclysmic battle between good and evil, the last and severest test of humanity's allegiance to God. In the light of this belief the Church has been led to pray: "And do not subject us to the final test, but deliver us from the evil one" (Matthew 6:13). Perhaps the memory of Jesus in the wilderness confirmed the Church's faith that the ultimate victory would belong to God; Jesus' experience proved this. Not only would the image of Jesus in the desert somehow focus Israel's long history of struggle, temptation, and learning to live the ways of God. Not only does Jesus in the desert demonstrate fidelity where Israel had many times failed. Not only does Jesus' experience of temptation and his renunication of Satan somehow redeem and reclaim the historical experience of his people. But also what Jesus undergoes signals to his followers that they too will be drawn into the struggle against the powers of darkness, precisely because of their association with him. His experience is a preview of what the Church down through the centuries will likewise experience as it continually renounces Satan. The memory of Jesus in the wilderness can strengthen the pilgrim people of God from one generation to the next and invigorate their faith in the abiding power of God over evil.

The disciples had undoubtedly learned that by themselves they were no match for the power of evil. It had caught them the night on which Jesus was betrayed, abandoned, and vehemently denied. They had been seized with fear of being caught with Jesus. They, the chosen ones, had run for their lives, abandoning Jesus in the garden to the devil who had departed from him in the desert, but only, as Luke remarked, "for a time" (Luke 4:13). At the Last Supper Jesus said, "Simon, Simon, behold Satan has demanded to sift all of you like wheat, but I have prayed that your own faith may not fail; and once you have turned back, you must strengthen your brothers" (Luke 22:31–32). The disciples would have always remembered their experience of "being sifted." Their faith had not been strong enough to overcome their fear of death, even though it would have meant dying alongside the Son of God. But this sorry realization of their own cowardice and fear would never have occurred if they had not been drawn into Jesus' company. It would have been impossible to travel with Jesus and not come face to face with their inner poverty. The memory of the disciples in flight can keep the Church earnest and humble when it prays, "But deliver us from the evil one."

Matthew and Luke elaborate the desert episode. What lay at the core of Jesus' temptation in the wilderness? To bend the power and will of God to suit human plans. In each of the three scenes in the desert, the tempter acts to entice Jesus to grab power, to demonstrate that he had divine approval, to prove that he had God in his pocket. The parallel with Adam becomes clear. Adam had been seduced by the prospect that he would be like God: in the garden Adam reached for the divine likeness, as he falsely imagined it, and he fell from grace. But Jesus in the wilderness was not misled. Matthew writes:

Scene One: He fasted for forty days and forty nights, and afterwards he was hungry. The tempter approached and said to him, "If you are the Son of God, command that these stones become loaves of bread." He said in reply, "It is written: 'One does not live by bread alone, but by every word that comes forth from the mouth of God.' " (4:2–4)

Scene Two: Then the devil took him to the holy city, and made him stand on the parapet of the temple, and said to him, "If you are the Son of God, throw yourself down. For it is written: 'He will command his angels concerning you' and 'with their hands they will support you, lest you dash your foot against a stone.' " Jesus answered him, "Again it is written, 'You shall not put the Lord, your God, to the test.' " (4:5–7)

Scene Three: Then the devil took him up to a very high mountain, and showed him all the kingdoms of the world in their magnificence, and he said to him, "All these I shall give to you, if you will prostrate yourself and worship me." At this, Jesus said to him, "Get away, Satan! It is written: 'The Lord, your God, shall you worship and him alone shall you serve.' " (4:8–10)

Three times Jesus renounces Satan. Three times he rejects the glamor of evil, he refuses to be mastered by sin, and chooses to live in the freedom of the children of God. Before we can fruitfully meditate on the significance of these scenes, we ought to recall that the accounts of Jesus' baptism and temptation are positioned by Matthew, Mark, and Luke at the beginning of his public life. They are not independent of the events and teaching which follow. Whatever Jesus is rejecting has to do with the nature and purpose of his mission. Indeed, Jesus refuses to change stones into bread in order to satisfy a forty-day hunger; but we miss the point if we think that Jesus, out of humility, is refusing to show off, or to use divine power for his own advantage. The point is not that Jesus had such power but refused to use it. The gospel does not say that Jesus could have turned stones into bread if he wanted to. Rather, the devil mistakenly believes that being Son of God must mean that Jesus has unconditional divine power at his disposal, whereas being Son of God entailed no such thing. In fact, if we follow Mark's story to the end, being Son of God means something very different. In

Mark's account, it was the centurion at the foot of the cross who finally and correctly identified Jesus as the Son of God, in his moment of absolute emptiness (Mark 15:39). Being Son of God means being poor, being betrayed and abandoned, being powerless and victimized—conditions which we ordinarily do not think of when imagining what it must be like to be Son of God. Certainly, Adam—who was deceived into thinking that equality with God was something he should grasp—would never have guessed such a thing.

Jesus, like some of the Old Testament prophets, worked miracles. The Spirit of God rested upon the prophets, as it rested on Jesus, empowering them to speak and to act in God's name. But their having the Spirit never implied that they could act independently of God, and neither could Jesus. The faith vision which informs the fourth gospel confirms this point. According to John, Jesus only does what he sees the Father doing (John 5:19); he only speaks what he hears from the Father (8:28). Because he is the Son, Jesus never acts on his own, apart from the Father. Therefore, it would be wrong to suppose that Jesus possessed divine power unconditionally. Furthermore, everything we know about his life tells us that Jesus had emptied himself (Philippians 2:7): not only on the cross, but through a day by day self-emptying of which the cross is the last and most dramatic expression both of his powerlessness and of his absolute trust in God.

The devil, or Satan, is putting a stumbling block in Jesus' way. In Hebrew, "Satan" stands for "opponent," "adversary," or "stumbling block." It is the word Jesus used when he sharply rebuked Peter: "Get behind me, Satan!" (Mark 8:33). Whether we conceive Satan as some kind of personal spirit, like a fallen angel, or as a metaphor for the real presence of evil in the world, Satan is whatever is hostile to human well-being. Satan is whatever opposes us, preventing us from becoming fully human and free. By definition evil is whatever defaces the divine image and likeness which God has created in each of us. To be sure, in the gospels Jesus speaks as if Satan were a personal being. And the existence of such a being may help to explain the origin and presence of evil in the world and in human history. But belief in the existence of an Evil One creates as many problems as it solves. To some, it suggests that God and the devil are competing in the world for human allegiance and that the outcome is up for grabs. For others, given the horrible evils which human beings have inflicted on one another, the devil's power seems stronger than God's. Such people are more terrified by talk of Satan than consoled by talk of God.[4]

We probably should not infer too much from the fact that Jesus mentions Satan. The evangelists, and Jesus himself, expressed themselves within the religious imagination and cultural horizon of their day. Satan thus seemed to be a distinct personality. But whether evil originates in a devil as a personification of wickedness or in the selfish recesses of the human mind and heart ultimately makes little difference. The fact is that we do experience something which is contrary to the lifegiving movement of God in our lives and in the world. And this causes us to stumble, to lose our way, and to miss the mark in our journey to become fully daughters and sons of God. That Jesus had to struggle to remain faithful to his vision of the mission the Father had given him, there should be little doubt.

In the second and third scenes Satan raises the stakes dramatically. From the desert floor, to the pinnacle of the temple, and then finally to a very high mountain, the devil attempts to seduce Jesus to seize power in a way which would do violence to human freedom. The devil tempted him to win people's religious commitment by catering to their craving for the miraculous. People are so impressed by displays of power; why not perform all kinds of mighty signs and stun them into discipleship? Of what use is a messiah who cannot work wonders the way Moses did?

Or perhaps Jesus could be tricked into implementing his religious vision by winning people to himself and not to God. This is one of the most subtle and perverse temptations which those who believe themselves chosen by God can possibly face. The messenger begins to look for reassurance and approval from other men and women; increasingly he judges his success by their reaction to him. More and more the messenger operates out of his own deep need to feel accepted, and what could make anyone feel more accepted than to be recognized publicly as God's chosen instrument? In the process the messenger draws men and women to believe in him, to depend on him instead of on God.

Or maybe Jesus could be tempted to fulfill his mission by having it handed to him by the powers of darkness, that is, by compromising his loyalty to the Father. Jesus would then receive his licence to preach from political and religious authorities, whose interests he would never threaten. In that case he could teach and do whatever he wished, provided he did not infringe on the prerogatives of the public authorities or sensitize the crowds to their hypocrisy. But if he really is God's Son, which is what the devil wanted him to prove, then the depth of his trust in God would be the only adequate demonstration. Jesus' loyalty to the Father had to be absolute and unconditional.

Jesus was not to be deceived into believing that the kingdom of God would be advanced if he drew people to God by ungodlike means. To do so would be to subvert their faith and take advantage of their freedom. He would not exploit religiously gullible people, nor would he preach simply what men and women wanted to hear. Jesus would not bargain with any earthly power in order to make his way easier and safer, or to swell the number of his followers.

Throughout the scenes of the desert episode, Jesus himself is being tested. But as I said, these scenes are preparing us to understand the course of Jesus' ministry which is just beginning. As his public life unfolded, Jesus would undoubtedly keep praying and discerning God's will, since there would be voices—human voices, and some very close to home—which would try to deter Jesus from the path God was showing him. Mark's gospel, for example, preserves a memory that the relatives of Jesus, believing he was out of his mind, wanted to seize him (Mark 3:21). Luke recalls that the people in Jesus' home town took offense at his message and attempted to throw him off a cliff (Luke 4:29). And we remember how Peter took Jesus aside and began to rebuke him after Jesus had explained where his mission would lead (Matthew 16:22–23). Jesus had to keep on rejecting—and to teach his disciples that they must do the same—any path that would weaken their absolute trust in God and any means that would undermine human freedom. There would be no fire from heaven to destroy the ungracious towns (Luke 9:54), no miracles where people lacked faith (Mark 6:5), no winking at the hypocrisy of the rich or the ecclesiastical establishment (Matthew 23:13–36), no pampering of his disciples (Mark 8:14–21), no multiplying of loaves for political gain (John 6:15), no deals with political or religious authorities, or with prostitutes and tax-collectors, by which they could sidestep the full cost of conversion. Surely the disciples must have wondered at times whether there was not an easier route to the kingdom of God.

THE SIGNIFICANCE OF THE TEMPTATION STORY
Whatever the historical kernel behind them, the temptation scenes were shaped by the gospel writers, since

presumably Jesus was by himself in the desert. No one was there to record what the devil said, or to note the Old Testament quotations which Jesus employed in answering the devil. This point, of course, does not allow us to conclude that the gospel accounts are mere fabrications. One must simply acknowledge, with the best of New Testament scholarship, that the gospels are faith documents, not historical annals. The temptation episodes are reported, not for the sake of providing historical information, but in order to aid us in understanding the mission and person of Jesus.

It is unlikely that the evangelists intended to suggest a correspondence between Jesus' temptation in the wilderness and those we may undergo at times. The struggle reflected in those desert scenes concerns Jesus as Messiah; whatever temptations we experience are not of a messianic nature. We cannot be tempted the way Jesus was because none of us is called to be the one who takes away the sin of the world. Nevertheless, the temptation story elucidates the ministry and mission of Jesus. And since we are baptized into the life, death, and resurrection of Jesus, we, like him, will be tested. Like him, we must learn how to recognize and reject what is untrue.

The reason for including the temptation account in the gospel narrative is not merely to teach us that because Jesus is human he is tempted, just as we are. That much is fairly obvious. According to the Letter to the Hebrews, ". . . we do not have a high priest who is unable to sympathize with our weaknesses, but one who has similarly been tested in every way, yet without sin" (Hebrews 4:15). The implication here is that Jesus was drawn into our experience of being tempted and tested, which includes the temptation to be unfaithful to God. But we struggle against sin as men and women whose spirits are already weakened, not only by our own personal sinfulness, but also by the sinfulness around us. Jesus, on the other hand, faced temptation as one whose spirit is intimately joined to the Father. Thus he did not react to temptation with the murky indecision and confused intention which characterize so much of our thinking and acting. He understood temptation out of the clarity and sensitivity of someone whose entire self lived and existed for God. He experienced temptation with the uncompromised freedom of one who is fully a child of God.

Jesus rejected sin, therefore, not as someone who was afraid of the consequences, afraid of being punished or of losing his Father's approval. Rather, since he lived out of an intense faith and love, he grasped temptation as only a man or woman of God would. For him, yielding to temptation and thus committing sin amounted to nothing less than turning aside from what he believed to be the Father's will. As a result of his testing, Jesus "learned obedience from what he suffered . . . and was made perfect" (Hebrews 5:8–9). In other words, Jesus became fully free, fully alive, and fully a believer; and thus he became the source of our freedom, our life, our belief, and our "eternal salvation." As a believer, Jesus too had to pray, to seek God's will, and to discern what the Father was asking of him. This suggests that we should regard his temptation in the wilderness against the wider background of a continual effort at discerning what the Father wanted him to do. Temptation to sin is not the only form which spiritual struggle and testing can take.

This description of temptation and sin might sound pious and overly simplified to us; but if it does, then that is only because our minds and wills are so habitually unfocussed and so easily swayed. We believe that it is normal or even natural for human beings to be confused about their motives and desires. Thus, we automatically defend our confusion, our moral ambivalence, or our spiritual sluggishness, by pleading that we are, after all, only human. Satan could not pull Jesus away from God because Jesus was (and is) fully human, fully free and alive. He demonstrated what is really "natural" about being human, which is to pursue a course toward the Father under the direction and power of the Spirit.

How then might we describe the difference between Jesus' temptation and ours? Because he was the Son, perhaps Jesus' vulnerability lay in the possibility of taking a route toward the kingdom which avoided poverty, rejection, humiliation, powerlessness, and death. But our vulnerability lies in the insecurity and fear which lead us to cover up what we really are. It lies in our impatience, or in our appetite for having the upper hand or the last word, or in our insensitivity to things of the Spirit, or in our reluctance to be alone with God. For the follower of Jesus, however, this description can be specified further. The disciple is drawn into a life-long wrestling against sin precisely because of his or her effort at being faithful to Jesus. In other words, it is the gospel that reveals the nature of temptation in Christian life. Good and evil, for us, are defined by the teaching and example of Jesus, that is by his life, death, and resurrection. Whatever would prevent us from being like him, therefore, is harming the image of God which each of us is called to realize. That is where the power of sin reveals itself in our experience. The temptations we endure consist of those desires, circumstances, and possibilities which would separate us from Jesus; and we fail whenever we choose a path other than the one which Jesus himself followed.

THE BAPTISMAL QUESTIONS
The formula through which the church asks us to reject Satan is crisp and to the point: "Do you reject Satan, and all his works, and all his empty promises?" This can be elaborated in a second series of questions: "Do

you reject sin, so as to live in the freedom of God's children? Do you reject the glamor of evil, and refuse to be mastered by sin? Do you reject Satan, father of sin and prince of darkness?" In one way or another, these questions boil down to the same thing: Do you recognize the reality of sin and evil, and are you determined, with God's help, to refuse it any entry into your life?

It should be abundantly clear that we cannot think of rejecting Satan without recalling the story of Jesus in the desert. His experience in the wilderness sets the stage for our promising to reject Satan, his works, and his empty promises. The Church suggests as much by assigning this gospel reading to the First Sunday of Lent, at the beginning of our seasonal preparation for renewing our baptismal promises at the Easter Vigil. Jesus refused Satan any room in his thinking and choosing. He exposed the devil's temptation to change stones into bread for the deception that it was. Miraculous signs which proceeded from any motive except the desire to serve God would be displays of power for its own sake, and hence a work of the Evil One. Whatever God's servant does must reflect the presence and Spirit of God; the servant does not serve his own interests, but God's. Jesus saw right through the devil's suggestion that he throw himself down from a high place in order to test God's love and power. What would that prove? This would not be a sign of anything except a lack of absolute trust in God on Jesus' part. It would prove to Satan's satisfaction that Jesus was not the Son, because the Son would not feel it necessary to test his Father's care. And Jesus was not fooled by Satan's promise to deliver him the nations of the world, if only he would prostrate before the devil and worship him. The nations of the world were not Satan's to give, but if Jesus betrayed God then all would be lost, and the world would then indeed belong to the Evil One.

While these temptations clearly bear on Jesus' role as Messiah, it is important for us to think about them. Satan was tempting Jesus to abandon the path his Father had marked out for him. We are not called to be messiahs, but we are called to follow Jesus. As a result, the path the Father directed him to take has enormous consequences for the way we live. The disciples of Jesus will certainly be caught up in the mystery of power being made perfect through weakness. For us the overriding question in our lives has to be: Will I be loyal to Jesus? This is what rejecting Satan means.

The baptismal questions about rejecting Satan can be reduced to one basic question about our renewed readiness to renounce whatever is not of God in our lives. To spell out in detail what this implies would require a careful review of the gospels themselves, because there the life and teaching of Jesus reveal what obeying God and rejecting evil mean. In general, whatever harms or destroys human beings, whatever threatens their dignity as sons and daughters of God, is evil. Through sinful actions men and women can destroy the image and likeness of God which they are. By sinning, they forfeit their freedom and become slaves to people, to things, or to situations which rob them of their humanity.

Two things in particular stand out in Jesus' teaching: the need to forgive and the danger of wealth. Both of these concern human freedom, since the one who cannot forgive, like the person who needs to hear the word of forgiveness, remains unfree, locked into anger, or guilt, or resentment, or fear. And the person who remains attached to money cannot love and serve God. Money demands service. It needs to be protected and cleverly invested. It needs to be on good terms with the right friends. In our culture, many people want to be rich without worrying about the social or human cost. Often financial success is achieved at the expense of other people, of relationships, or of the poor. People develop class loyalties; they work together to protect their interests. Greed is renamed competition, and what fuels the economic order is nothing less than an unbridled desire to own, to display, and to consume material goods.

Jesus' teaching about wealth is one of the strongest features of the gospel story, as a moment's reflection will verify. "How hard it is for those who have wealth to enter the kingdom of God!" And Jesus continued, "It is easier for a camel to pass through the eye of a needle than for one who is rich to enter the kingdom of God" (Mark 10:23, 25). That text will not be silenced. The one who serves money (and all that money represents) is radically unfree, although frequently unaware of it. Our manner of living betrays us. While they might not admit it, the sad fact is that many Christians seem to be looking for the formula which would allow them to serve both God and money, on the outside chance that Jesus may have been exaggerating when he said, "No servant can serve two masters. He will either hate the one and love the other, or be devoted to one and despise the other. You cannot serve God and mammon" (Luke 16:13). The glamor of money can be imprisoning. Through mammon sin demonstrates its power to master human beings. It must be rejected, firmly and decisively.

The problem is that evil does not usually carry a banner announcing itself. If we perceived evil for what it is, we would run away from its imprisoning reach. Evil generally masks itself as something good and desirable, or else it turns something which is genuinely good into something sinful by urging us to do the right thing for the wrong reason. That, of course, was Satan's tactic with Jesus; that is what temptations are all about. It is not always easy to recognize when we are truly serving God and when we are merely serving ourselves. The

36

Christian tradition has long acknowledged this problem, and that is why experts in the way of the Spirit advise prayer, fasting, almsgiving, and discernment. It is hardly accidental that Jesus' victory over Satan in the wilderness was preceded by an extensive period of prayerful solitude and fasting. Evil is not easily uncovered from its glamorous wrappings, so smoothly does it insinuate itself into our thoughts, desires, and affections. Prayerful discernment, therefore, has to be a lifelong process. The disciple needs to come before the Lord regularly, meditating on his words and example, and asking for self-knowledge and spiritual insight. We need continually to clarify for ourselves what our lives are about, what we are really seeking and serving, what we fear, and where our loyalties lie. We need every now and then a wilderness season like Lent, a period of greater prayer and penance which demonstrates our seriousness about following Jesus and our determination to discern carefully what the Lord is asking of us.

WHAT ARE WE RENOUNCING?
St. Cyril of Jerusalem, writing in the fourth century, explained the significance of the baptismal promises to those who were readying themselves for Christian initiation: "I renounce you, Satan, you wicked and cruel tyrant; I no longer . . . fear your power. For Christ broke that power by sharing flesh and blood with me, planning . . . to break, by His death, the power of death, to save me from subjection to perpetual bondage. I renounce you, crafty scoundrel of a serpent; I renounce you, traitor, perpetrator of every crime, who inspired our first parents to revolt. I renounce you, Satan, agent and abettor of all wickedness."

Cyril continued: "Then in a second phrase you are taught to say, 'and all your works.' All sin is the 'works of Satan'; and sin, too, you must renounce, since he who has escaped from a tyrant has also cast off the tyrant's livery. Sin in all its forms, then, is included in the works of the Devil. Only let me tell you this: all your words, particularly those spoken at this awful hour, are recorded in the book of God. Whenever, therefore, you are caught in conduct contrary to your profession, you will be tried as a renegade. Renounce, then, the works of Satan, that is, every irrational deed and thought.

"Next you say, 'and all his pomp.' The pomp of the Devil is the craze for the theater, the horse races in the circus, the wild-beast hunts, and all such vanity . . . Avoid an addiction to the theater, with its spectacle of licentiousness, the lewd and unseemly antics of actors and the frantic dancing of degenerates . . . After this you say, 'and all your service.' The service of the Devil is prayer in the temple of idols, the honoring of lifeless images . . ."[5]

The renunication of sin and the devil had, it is easy to see, assumed an expression which is close to the formula the Church still uses at its Easter Vigil service. But Cyril, good teacher that he was, realized that people needed to be made fully aware of what they were giving up. Were he alive today, he would probably tell the candidates for baptism that they must avoid things like pornographic movies and books, compulsive gambling, boxing, and whatever caters to the human appetite for violence. He would spell out contemporary forms of idolatry and name the various false gods which men and women today are serving. He might go on to specify the many forms which pride, avarice, and the thirst for power have taken in modern society. He could speak about lying, manipulation, racism, and the loss of an effective sense of justice.

The contemporary political and social situation would offer him a lot of grist for his catechetical mill. Cyril might quote, in fact, from documents like Vatican II's Pastoral Constitution on the Church in the Modern World, or *The Challenge of Peace* and *Economic Justice for All*, two of the recent pastoral letters written by the bishops of the United States. "The arms race," he would say, quoting the council, "is an utterly treacherous trap for humanity, and one which injures the poor to an intolerable degree."[6] Enormous profits are to be made through manufacturing and selling weapons: the money does not wind up helping the poor, and the weapons often wind up being used to kill and oppress them. The root of this evil is greed, and that sin rests on many a national conscience. Or he might have cited the teaching of Paul VI, which was quoted by the U.S. bishops: "Private property does not constitute for anyone an absolute or unconditioned right. No one is justified in keeping for his exclusive use what he does not need, when others lack necessities."[7]

On the positive side, Cyril might urge his catechumens to do their part in promoting justice and respect for human life. In fact, he could ask them to read Matthew 25 and to meditate on the scene of the last judgment where the unrighteous are condemned because they did not recognize Jesus in the faces of the imprisoned, or the hungry, or the stranger who needs shelter. Surely, Cyril would instruct them about the higher righteousness which Jesus expects of his followers: they are not to swear, or to indulge lustful thoughts, or to harbor a grudge. They are, in fact, to be perfect, as their heavenly Father is perfect (Matthew 5:48).

When Jesus speaks of perfection, he is using a term that corresponds to the Hebrew word "wholeness" or "integrity." Our love of God is whole or complete when our love for our neighbor flows out of our love for God. There is, at least for Christians, no route to God that bypasses our neighbor. "And who is my neighbor?" (Luke 10:29) The neighbor is always the one who needs me here and now. Jesus did not define the neighbor in terms of the person or family living next door. Instead, he defined the neighbor socially and politically as the one (or the group, or the class, or the nation) who here and now confronts us out of hunger, or poverty, or brokenness: the refugee or exile, those who have been victimized, or who lack the human and spiritual resources to put their lives back together. We only have to read the newspaper or to watch television to discover who our neighbors are. Christian morality, therefore, can never be a private affair between the disciple and Jesus, or between the individual believer and God. The ethics governing Christian existence includes a radical challenge to be involved in the life of the human community.

THE "POSITIVE" ASPECT OF TEMPTATION
It is worth reminding ourselves that there can be some spiritual advantage to the experience of being tempted. With marvelous insight Teilhard de Chardin wrote: "What feeble powers and bloodless hearts Your creatures would bring You if they were to succeed in cutting themselves off prematurely from the providential setting in which You have placed them!"[8] He means that men and women will not come to their full stature as human beings if they keep trying to escape the burdens and challenges of their humanness. Our coming of age depends upon our dealing maturely and courageously with the forces and tensions of the concrete situation in which we live from day to day. Not every tension that arises in our lives is a temptation to evil. Many of these tensions help us to grow as intelligent and free people. They arise from our work, our study, our having to acquire basic human virtues like patience and tact, our remaining faithful to one another, our worries about our children, or about the conditions of our country and the world, and so forth.

But temptation sometimes constitutes a large part of our daily struggle. If Jesus' example in the wilderness means anything, then we have to say at the very least that being tempted characterizes the human condition; no one, not even the Son of God, is exempt. In fact, to repeat a point made earlier, since it was the Spirit who led Jesus into the desert, we have to say that often temptation begins after the Spirit is given to us. Or perhaps we should say *because* the Spirit has been given to us. The struggle which the disciples of Jesus experience stems from their having come to know him. If we had not begun to understand his example and teaching, to accept his values and to share his faith, or if we had not been drawn into the mystery of his dying and rising and promised to follow him, then our spirit would have experienced much less tension, and probably much less growth.

Temptation is inevitably part of Christian life, not just because as human beings we are prone to sin, but because we have shared in the Spirit of Jesus. The Spirit itself draws us to confront the power of evil in the concrete circumstances of our lives. And if the Spirit is drawing us, then in the experience of struggle our belief should be reconfirmed that nothing ultimately can frustrate God's creative design. Maybe this is what Paul had in mind when he wrote: "We know that all things work for good for those who love God, who are called according to his purpose" (Romans 8:28). In our case, as well as in the case of Jesus, there would be little possibility of becoming perfect without the experience of being tested.

God's *creative* design. The Spirit who marks out for each of us his or her own personal desert or wilderness is also the creator Spirit who hovers over the waters of chaos in the opening chapter of the Book of Genesis. There are periods of our lives, after all, when we feel as if we are wandering in a wilderness, or as if we are being pulled and tested, or as if God is as dry and unappetizing as the desert sand. The desert can be any place, and we may have to pass through that place many times. Without faith, none of us would be able to see that place for what it is, namely, the place where our spirit and God's Spirit meet.

The Spirit who draws us into the wilderness—an especially appropriate image for seasons like Advent and Lent—is the same Spirit who creates us, continually. There are times, therefore, when we should interpret our experience of temptation as an experience of being made or fashioned more closely into the image and likeness of God. This is particularly true when the struggle would never have arisen unless we had first come to know and love Christ. Putting on Christ, who is for us the divine likeness, never happens without our feeling the pressure of God's hand molding and forming us. That hand stretches and shapes our capacity for faith, for compassion, for hope and perseverance; it enhances our freedom and purifies our humanity, even though we may not be aware that it is God's power we are feeling.

Of course, this does not happen apart from our daily rejection of Satan, his works, and all his empty promises. This daily saying-no exercises our soul's deepest possibilities. If in our search for peace we were to succeed in separating ourselves from every occasion or condition where our spirit has to wrestle against the power of evil, then we would soon turn into feeble creatures with bloodless hearts. When Jesus taught his followers to pray "Lead us not into temptation," he was not instructing them to ask God to keep them from being tempted altogether, but rather to save them from the great test, "the terrible outbreak of moral chaos and violence just before the end, when the powers of evil would seem to gain the upper hand over the disciples."9

This is apocalyptic language, that is, it derives from expectations about the end of the world and the final battle between good and evil. We do not generally think or pray in such terms today. "Lead us not into temptation" sounds a bit different from "Do not bring us to the test." And, "Deliver us from evil" does not quite mean "Keep us from ever having to face our own sinfulness." Why not hear these words of the Our Father against the background of Paul's idea that all of creation is groaning for liberation (Romans 8:18ff.)? They are words to be prayed with eager expectation and longing. Such prayers for liberation do not implore God to let us escape being tested and challenged; rather, they resound with confidence and hope. Through them we speak to the God who will one day rescue creation from its bondage to death and decay. We shall certainly face temptation, but just as certainly, if we stand fast with Christ, we shall grow into the freedom of the children of God.

NOTES

1. St. Ambrose, *Theological and Dogmatic Works*, trans. Roy J. Deferrari (Washington, D.C.: Catholic University of America Press, 1963), pp. 271 and 270. [This is volume 44 in the series *The Fathers of the Church*.]

2. G. W. H. Lampe notes: "The Baptism of Jesus was proleptic, signifying and summing up in a single action the entire mission and saving work of the Servant-Messiah, which was to be unfolded and revealed gradually in the course of His life, death, resurrection, and ascension." See *The Seal of the Spirit* (London: S.P.C.K., 1967), p. 45. And Jon Sobrino remarks: "The temptations have to do with Jesus himself, with what is most basic to his person and his mission. That is why they are placed alongside the account of Jesus' baptism, for Christian theological reflection saw his baptism as Jesus' decision to accept his mission from God. Temptation is the general atmosphere in which Jesus grows and develops, as is the case with every human being. It is not a matter of choosing between good and evil but of choosing between two very different ways of conceiving and carrying out his mission, of using power, of picturing God, and of rendering the kingdom present to people." *Christology at the Crossroads* (Maryknoll, N.Y.: Orbis Books, 1978), p. 365.

3. From the *Testament of Naphtali*, as quoted by D. E. Nineham, *Saint Mark* (Philadelphia: Westminster Press, 1963), p. 64.

4. See the entry under "Satan" in *The Interpreter's Dictionary of the Bible*, volume 4 (Nashville: Abingdon Press, 1962), pp. 224–228.

5. Leo P. McCauley, S.J. and Anthony A. Stephenson, trans., *The Works of Saint Cyril of Jerusalem*, volume 2 (Washington, D.C.: Catholic University of America Press, 1970), pp. 155–157. [This is volume 64 in the series *The Fathers of the Church*.] In similar fashion, St. John Chrysostom also elaborated the moral dimensions of baptism. See his *Baptismal Instructions*, trans. Paul Harkins (Westminster, Md.: Newman Press, 1963). [This is volume 31 in the Ancient Christian Writers Series.]

6. The Pastoral Constitution on the Church in the Modern World, #81. See *The Documents of Vatican II*, ed. Walter M. Abbott (New York: Herder & Herder, Association Press, 1966), p. 295. Throughout this book, quotations from Vatican II documents are taken from Abbott's edition of the texts.

7. *Economic Justice for All*, #115.

8. Pierre Teilhard de Chardin, *The Divine Milieu: An Essay on the Interior Life* (New York: Harper & Row, 1960), p. 82.

9. John P. Meier, *Matthew* (Wilmington: Michael Glazier, 1980), p. 62.

Chapter Two

Do You Believe in God, the Father Almighty, Creator of Heaven and Earth?

In the beginning, when God created the heavens and the earth, the earth was a formless wasteland, and darkness covered the abyss, while a mighty wind swept over the waters.

Genesis 1:1–2

Hear, O Israel! The Lord is our God, the Lord alone! Therefore, you shall love the Lord, your God, with all your heart, and with all your soul, and with all your strength.

Deuteronomy 6:4–5

When Israel was a child I loved him, out of Egypt I called my son. . . . I drew them with human cords, with bands of love; I fostered them like one who raises an infant to his cheeks. Yet, though I stooped to feed my child, they did not know that I was their healer.

Hosea 11:1, 4

The formula by which we renounce the devil appears to correspond to the questions through which we profess our faith. We are asked, "Do you reject Satan?" The corresponding question is, "Do you believe in God the Father Almighty, creator of heaven and earth?" Because we believe in the Father, the one who creates, we necessarily reject whatever is contrary to the divine creative action in our lives and in the world. To believe in God, however, means more than working against sinfulness. It also means leading lives of praise, reverence, and service.

The next part of the renunciation formula asks, "And all his works?" The corresponding question of faith is, "Do you believe in Jesus Christ, his only Son, our Lord, who was born of the Virgin Mary, was crucified, died, and was buried, rose from the dead, and is now seated at the right hand of the Father?" In short, do we accept the whole mystery of Christ—the life, ministry, death, and glorification of Jesus? Believing in this mystery is equivalent to accepting the works of God, as revealed to us through the life of Jesus: "This is the work of God, that you believe in the one he sent" (John 6:29). One thing is sure: this question cannot be answered merely by nodding assent. The practical side of this belief (and therefore the real answer to the faith-question) is our living as disciples, which obviously includes rejecting the counter-kingdom of Satan's works.

Finally, we have been asked whether we reject all the devil's empty promises. The only way we can answer that affirmatively is through the Holy Spirit, which Jesus promised to send us (John 15:26): the Spirit of truth who liberates us from insecurity and fear and presses us toward life. The corresponding question of faith is, "Do you believe in the Holy Spirit, the holy Catholic Church, the communion of saints, the forgiveness of sins, the resurrection of the body, and life everlasting?" Each of these are Spirit-realities. Spirit makes church possible; it is the bond of our union and the source of our common life. In fact, the Spirit *is* our common life, the same life which breathed through the heart and mind, the imagination and decisions, the freedom and love of Jesus. Spirit creates the "communion of saints," that is, the relationship between us and those pilgrims of faith who have preceded us. Spirit is what Jesus breathed on his disciples when he missioned them to continue his ministry of forgiveness and reconciliation. Spirit will raise our bodies to be with Christ.

Spirit is the very life of God, everlasting life, which has already begun among us. To believe in the Spirit, the promise of the Father, is therefore to reject the counterfeit promises of the father of lies (John 8:44).

A REFLECTION ON THE TRANSFIGURATION

Just as we allowed the temptation story to lead us into considering what it means to reject Satan, so in this chapter we start with the readings for the Second Sunday of Lent about the transfiguration of Jesus (Matthew 17:1–9; Mark 9:2–10; Luke 9:28–36). This dramatic interlude in the gospel narratives makes us think back to the accounts of Jesus' baptism. For here again there is a voice from heaven—the Father's voice—which declares, "This is my beloved Son, with whom I am well pleased." Then the voice adds, "Listen to him!" (Matthew 17:5). Like the temptation episode, this scene also carries a great deal of theological significance, although its historical background probably cannot be determined. The story may in fact be a resurrection scene which has been read back into the ministry of Jesus.[1] This should neither surprise nor distract us, however, because the gospels were written from the viewpoint of resurrection faith. The evangelists believed from the first stroke of their pens that Jesus, whose story they were telling, was the risen Lord. The Jesus of John's gospel, in fact, often sounds as if he is permanently transfigured; he seems to be speaking through the faith of a community which knows him to be now glorified.

As we move prayerfully through the Lenten season, we may need to catch a glimpse of Jesus' glory in order to sustain our penitential practice and our good works. This memory will be especially important as we move into the dark, sad moments of Jesus' suffering and death. The transfiguration reminds us, inside or outside the Lenten season, that the Jesus whom the evangelists were writing about was the Jesus who had been raised from the dead. It is the same Jesus whom we are following day by day. The voice which says "Listen to him!" is not only addressing Peter, James, and John; above all, it is speaking to us who read or hear the gospel story. This Jesus, whose inner reality has momentarily become clear to the disciples, is the Son, the one especially loved by the Father. What else does "Son" mean, what other definition could the word have, except one who has been loved, who has been chosen (Luke 9:35), and who has pleased God? For the Father has eyes only for the Son; the Father can only see Jesus. Jesus is truly the Son because he behaves like the Son. And this means that unless we become like Christ, God will not "see" us.

Through its recounting in the Church's Lenten liturgy, then, the transfiguration story takes on particular spiritual significance for us. While most of our images of Jesus are drawn from the down-to-earth scenes of the gospels, and we readily picture Jesus in everyday situations and circumstances, the fact is that the Jesus who lives in those scenes, who stirs our imaginations, and who draws us into the circle of his followers, is the living Lord. The more intimately we know him, the more likely we are to experience moments of transfiguration in which the underlying mystery—the inner reality—of our lives becomes clear. Ordinary situations, the people we live or work with everyday, the simple, routine things we have to do which absorb so much energy and attention, these are our route to God. There is no bypassing the everydayness, the tedium, the sheer familiarity involved in being human. No matter how much we hanker for novelty and excitement, sooner or later each situation becomes like the one before it. New faces become old faces, or they become just faces. Initially exciting activities turn into routines. We get used to things, to people, to ourselves, even to our relationship with God. In much the same way, perhaps, the disciples got used to Jesus, no matter how much he intrigued and excited them at first.

Yet occasionally, in the midst of everything, thanks to God's grace we see our lives with astonishing freshness. We catch sight of things from a perspective which throws into relief the worthwhileness of our lives, the humanness of the people around us, or the reason why we put up with so many things without complaint. Suddenly we remember why we made the choices we did, or the promises we made, or how deeply we love someone. Perhaps we grasp once again with amazing clarity the great Johannine insight that there is no point in professing to love a God we cannot see if we fail to love the brother or sister whom we do see (1 John 4:20). For the Christian there should be no radical disjunction between the kingdom of God and everyday life. Jesus was not a prayerful ascetic who lived in some barren wilderness or in the rarefied atmosphere of a mountain retreat. That would have suggested divine separateness, not a God who desired to come close to us. The followers of Jesus do not approach God immediately and directly by leading an existence totally uninterrupted by other men and women, or by the business of living. But the mystery of God needs to break into our routines now and then to rekindle this insight.

God loves the world (which means, God loves human beings) so much that, in Jesus, God joined the human story. Thus, the kingdom of God is in our midst (Luke 17:21). Jesus has so closely identified with us and with our concerns that now the mystery of God has penetrated everything. As its closeness is revealed, the mystery of God transfigures human life; people can know the nearness of God. Through faith, they experience the hand of God in their lives. They learn how to interpret suffering. Through faith, they realize that the future should be welcomed, not dreaded; and once their hearts have mastered the meaning of sacrifice, there is no limit to their love or their readiness to find the good in others.

The transfiguration story, then, is about the reality of God rushing into the ordinariness of human life and illuminating that silent mystery which has been accompanying us on our journey. It is about things being turned inside out, as when the disciples caught sight of the familiar Jesus from a totally new perspective. Jesus constantly lived and walked in the Father's presence, but with the transfiguration the hidden ground of Jesus' life came to the fore. He was the Son, whose proper place was with the Father. And as I suggested, from time to time our lives may be transfigured and their deeper meaning momentarily revealed. We are people whose proper place is to be with Jesus. The sudden perception of how real and how close the mystery of God is can overwhelm us and leave us speechless with gratitude.

Yet there is a second point to consider too. As Christians we call God Father because that is how Jesus knew and addressed God. Other people besides Christians have also conceived of God as a father, but for us the point is not so much the proper way of imaging God. Rather, the important matter is that there is a difference between knowing God with Jesus and knowing God apart from him. Many people have known God without ever having heard of Jesus. The first disciples, for example, believed in God before they met Jesus. Jesus, however, spoke of God as his father dearest—his *Abba*—and he thereby gave the title "father" a content which struck his disciples profoundly. Behind the word *Abba* stood the whole range of Jesus' experience of God. Jesus' teaching, activity, and example proceeded from his knowledge and experience of God, whom he called Father. It is his relationship with God that alone makes his life and ministry intelligible.

But the disciples also discovered something further. They learned that the only way they could come to know God as Jesus did was to be in the company of Jesus. Their experience of God as Father would be contingent upon their being with Jesus. The disciples discovered God in Jesus, and so, properly speaking, for them (and for the Church) God would always be the Father of our Lord Jesus Christ, the one who raised Jesus from the dead (Galatians 1:1). This is a major element of Christian belief. It helps us to locate some of the basis for our trinitarian faith within the religious experience of the disciples. It also prepares us to listen carefully to the transfiguration story, where the Father speaks of Jesus as "my beloved Son." The Father directed the disciples to listen to Jesus, just as during his ministry Jesus had been teaching them about the Father. And lest we think that the God whom Jesus revealed was discontinuous with the God who had been speaking through Israel's history, Moses and Elias appear there with him. They are talking about the suffering and death which await Jesus in Jerusalem, as if to suggest that nothing which happened to Jesus would fall outside God's providential plan, a lesson which the disciples apparently soon forgot (see Luke 24:25–27, 44–45). However startled men and women might have been with the authority and newness of Jesus' teaching (Mark 1:27), the transfiguration scene is clearly telling us that the God whom Jesus served and addressed as Father was the God of the prophets, the God of Moses and the Law, the God who created the heavens and the earth.

BELIEF AS ACTION

We should pause briefly to think about the first part of the faith-question, "Do you believe?" The full answer to this is "I do believe." *I* believe: that is to say, the whole person that I am, with all my talent, my energy, my love, my accomplishments and dreams, and my intelligence; and, yes, with all my hesitations, my blind spots, my likes and dislikes, my history of sinfulness, and my insecurity. This is the person who says, "Yes, I do believe." This is my self, the self that freely and maturely answers the Church's question. With a decision in freedom which is completely and unequivocally my own, I throw myself into this act of faith. With whatever measure of insight and freedom I have, I commit my self, my person, to the faith of the Christian community. *I* believe in God!

I *believe*. Believing implies trust, surrender, and acceptance. Belief is not the contrary of knowledge or reason, since even much of what we know rationally and scientifically we accept on the basis of someone's telling us or teaching us. What the Church tells us, and what, for example, doctors or politicians tell us, are quite different in terms of content; but for most of us, the act of believing itself does not immediately appear to be qualitatively different. My point is that we should not neatly juxtapose faith and reason, since natural, human trust plays a major role in the process of learning and thinking. Besides, there is a great deal of thinking and learning which accompanies the process of becoming fully believing Christians, and none of this takes place apart from God's grace. What distinguishes the two kinds of believing is that religious faith ultimately rests upon the word of God and is prompted by the Spirit, whereas ordinary human faith rests upon the word of other men and women. More specifically, faith in Jesus rests upon the scriptural word of God as proclaimed and lived by the believing community.

In his Letter to the Romans Paul wrote, "Thus faith comes from what is heard, and what is heard comes through the word of Christ" (Romans 10:17). Faith comes through hearing. In other words, our capacity for believing is awakened by the word and example of other believers, or by the Church's preaching, or by devout reading of Scripture, or by carefully attending to the silent mystery which surrounds our life and the lives of those around us. But what do we hear? We hear the word of God, although God obviously has neither lips nor voice. Still, we believe that God "speaks" to human beings. Sometimes the word of God is defined personally and applies to Jesus. Frequently it is defined in terms of written expression and applies to Scripture as a whole. And occasionally the word of God is defined socially or existentially and applies to anything in our experience which puts us in touch with the mystery of God. I think it can be argued that broadly speaking the word of God is whatever moves us away from selfishness, isolation, and sin, and towards freedom, community, and love. In short, we can define the word of God experientially as whatever makes us more fully human, or more completely daughters and sons of God.

Although the Church refers to Scripture as "the word of the Lord" and we call Jesus "the word made flesh," clearly what is of paramount importance is our ability to hear God speaking to us in and through Scripture, or in and through the life and teaching of Jesus, or in and through the Church's proclamation and the lives of other Christians. To hear the word of God precisely as God's word requires faith; it also presupposes God's grace. Otherwise we would not be able to perceive that it is God who is addressing us, nor would we be moved to respond through commitment and action. "No one can come to me," Jesus said, "unless the Father who sent me draw him" (John 6:44). Which is another way of saying that we could not recognize and respond to Jesus precisely as God's word without the Holy Spirit.

Where do we hear the word of God? If we answer, correctly, that we hear it in and through the believing community, then our faith still rests upon the word of other men and women. We accept their testimony, and much of our knowledge of faith comes to us this way. One generation passes the gospel message along to the next.

But there is something each generation includes as it passes the message along which goes beyond the verbal content. It is also testifying, "We have found this message to be lifegiving. Through this message we have discovered the freedom of the children of God." Like the townspeople who said to the woman whom Jesus had encountered at the well, "We no longer believe because of your word; for we have heard for ourselves, and we know that this is truly the Savior of the world" (John 4:42); so too do we come to accept the word which the Church teaches us. We believe, finally, because we trust our experience. If our faith is to be genuinely God-centered, then we simply have to trust the word of God which each of us can hear only in the silent depths of our hearts. The Church—the believing community—tells us about God; it preaches God's word. But faith eventually must go beyond the human testimony. However nourished we are by the Church's preaching, or by the charismatic witness which some Christians give; however reassured we are by accounts of the religious experience of saints, there is no avoiding the fact that if faith is to be truly adult, liberating, and lasting, then we have to know God for ourselves.

When we say, therefore, that we *believe*, we are first of all affirming, under the impulse of grace, the faith of the community and inserting ourselves into it. We are saying yes to its stories of faith, to its Scripture, and to the doctrines, values, and practices which identify it as Christian. But we are also admitting that our whole lives, basically, unfold in trusting surrender to the word of God, a word which we must daily listen for, and which each of us must hear for himself or herself. Yet this word never privatizes our faith, either. The word of God does not draw us into isolation or steep us in purely private relationships to God. Paradoxical as it may sound, that word, uttered and heard in silence, draws us into the circle of faith. It joins us in the Spirit with those who will become our sisters and brothers in the community of believers.

From time to time we articulate our faith, as, for example, when we renew our baptismal promises or recite the creed. We need to do this. We need to hear ourselves, and to let others hear us, state out loud what we actually believe. But this is just the surface or outward expression of hearts and minds which are always believing and trusting in God the Father of our Lord Jesus Christ. To be human means first and foremost to live in relationship to God. It is to be convinced that each breath we draw, every thought, word, or action of ours, depends upon the God who sustains us from one moment to the next. Nothing about us escapes God, because human existence is so deeply rooted in the divine mystery. By virtue of our creation we are in, from, and toward that holy mystery. The difference between believers and non-believers is that the believer recognizes this fundamental human fact and celebrates it. The believer hears the voice of God stirring irresistibly in the stillness of the human soul.

GOD, THE FATHER ALMIGHTY

Not only did Jesus call God "Father," but he instructed his disciples to do the same, and so, through the Spirit of God, we too can cry "*Abba*, Father!" (Romans 8:15). Although the word "father" is not sexually neutral, still the way God is Father is so different from the way men are fathers, that in fact the title transcends every human image or definition. God "the Father"—"from whom every family in heaven and on earth is named"

55

(Ephesians 3:15)—is part of our religious heritage because that is how Jesus addressed God. When Jesus calls God "Father," therefore, he is not measuring God according to a human standard. Rather, if anything, it is God who sets the standard for all human parenting. For Jesus, who compared himself to a hen gathering her young under her wings (Matthew 23:37), God was as truly mother as father; his conception of God was not determined by gender roles within first-century Jewish society. The way Jesus spoke about God, and the way God is portrayed through the whole life of Jesus, allows us to grasp why Jesus' way of addressing God as Father could sound revolutionary.[2] It implied a closeness to God unlike that shared by anyone else. We know that the word "*Abba,*" which Jesus used in referring to God, connotes intimacy, warmth, and childlike trust; it was a term of endearment. And Jesus invited his followers to address God as he did. To be able to say *Abba* ("Father") with Jesus is to share a new life, a life that makes us children of God.

In our profession of faith we would not be calling God our Father unless Jesus had instructed us to do so. "*Abba*, Father," is like a symbol embedded in the Christian consciousness. God would not be Father to us if we had not been drawn into a permanent relationship with Jesus. In other words, there is little point in addressing God as Father unless our spirits are united with Jesus. After all, he is the one who draws us to the Father, just as it is the Father who first drew us to Jesus (John 6:44). We may be aware of God without necessarily thinking about Jesus. We may in fact speak to the Father without imagining Jesus somehow standing alongside of us. Nevertheless, we would not be standing in God's presence at all if the Spirit of Jesus were not within us. Without Jesus, we simply do not know God, certainly not the God who was revealed to Jesus as "*Abba*, Father." Our faith rests upon the faith of

Jesus; otherwise, we should not be identified as Christians.

We ought to add a minor comment here. God is customarily referred to as the Father *Almighty*. "Almighty" may be calling attention to the majesty and holiness of God: " 'Holy, holy, holy is the Lord of hosts!' they cried one to the other. 'All the earth is filled with his glory!' " (Isaiah 6:3). Or, linking "Father" with "almighty" may be simply another way of saying that the God who is revealed as the Father of Jesus is none other than the God who created the heavens and the earth.

For many people calling God "Almighty Father" connotes power and strength, qualities which can sound somewhat onesided. These qualities need to be balanced in our liturgical and confessional language, as well as in our personal prayer, with other characteristics from Scripture and the Christian ascetical tradition which portray God as nurturing, as tender, as lover, and as co-sufferer. Otherwise, the richness of the way Jesus experienced and addressed God is too easily overshadowed by the very categories he had broken through. The God whom we confess to be all powerful is also the God who patiently and compassionately accompanies human beings throughout history. Indeed, the crucified Jesus remains a sign of this truth from one generation to the next. As Origen, one of the outstanding scripture scholars of the early church, commented:

"And also the Father himself, the God of all 'slow to anger and abounding in mercy' and compassionate, does he not in some way suffer? Don't you know when he directs human affairs he suffers human suffering? For 'the Lord your God bore your ways as a man bears his son.' Therefore God bears our ways just as the Son of God bears our sufferings. The very Father is not

without suffering. When he is prayed to, he has pity
and compassion; he suffers something of love and puts
himself in the place of those with whom he, in view of
the greatness of his nature, cannot be."[3]

CREATOR OF HEAVEN AND EARTH

What does it mean to believe that God has created the
heavens and the earth? The biblical writers never intel-
lectualized God into a philosophical principle which accounts for the existence of the world. In Scripture, God
is the one who creates, who judges, who shows mercy
and compassion; God bestows blessings, giving land
and offspring. God makes promises. God is the one
who governs the fortunes of nations and kingdoms,
who personally calls people, who raises up prophets
and kings, who liberates and ransoms. God is the one
who even raises the dead to life. In short, the biblical
God is known on the basis of divine action, and generations of human beings have witnessed the things God
has done among them.

The main issue here, however, is God's personal creation of each one of us. After all, creation is not merely
the physical and biological processes which form us.
Our creation involves all those personalizing and hu-
manizing forces which make us men and women who
are fully alive and fully free. If we believe that God is
truly our creator, then it becomes possible to appreciate
those forces as God's formative action in our lives. Like
the hand which shapes and molds the clay, people
sense the power of God moving in and through their
lives—in and through their very selves—and conform-
ing them to the likeness of Christ. We are people with
feelings and emotions. The circumstances, events, decisions, relationships, and so forth, in which we find
ourselves influence the direction of our growth and the
kind of person that we will become. In short, we are
people in the process of being made. And what exactly

is creating us? The answer to that is God, in whom we have said "I believe."

Our real self—the self that will last through eternity—is still being formed. The person which God calls each of us to be is still being fashioned. It cannot be otherwise. The second-century bishop and saint, Irenaeus, wrote:

" 'Could not God have displayed man perfect from the beginning?' If anyone asks this, he must be told that God is absolute and eternal, and in respect of himself all things are within his power. But contingent things have their beginning of being in the course of time, and for this reason *they must needs fall short of their maker's perfection;* for things which have recently come to birth cannot be eternal; and, not being eternal, they fall short of perfection for that very reason. *And being newly created they are therefore childish, and immature, and not yet fully trained for an adult way of life.* And so, just as a mother is able to offer food to an infant, but the infant is not yet able to receive food unsuited to its age; so God himself could have offered perfection to man at the beginning, but man, being yet an infant, *could not have taken it.*"[4]

Irenaeus' perspective is full of insight. Because we are living in time and space, and therefore subject to change, we cannot be what God intends us to be all at once. Consequently, our creation must stretch over a lifetime, according to the divine plan. Irenaeus does not allow himself to be distracted by the theoretical question: Could God have made us perfect from the outset? He concedes that God could have *offered* us perfection at the beginning, but what would have been the point? God did not make us with the capacity to accept perfection immediately.

What concerned Irenaeus, and what concerns us here and now, are those things which men and women experience. We are all well aware of being childish, immature, and not fully trained. We sense that we are in process, or pilgrims on a journey. We know temptation and struggle; we know how demanding it is to be faithful to Christ, to live up to our responsibilities, to be patient. Sometimes we seem to be moving backwards instead of advancing toward what Irenaeus calls the adult way of life. And yet, many times, the backwards movement actually serves to strengthen us by helping us rely upon God's mercy and love. In short, we did not emerge from the womb fully developed mentally, physically, and spiritually. We are human beings who in a very real sense are still being born, a fact which puzzled even a trained man like Nicodemus:

"Jesus answered and said to him, 'Amen, amen, I say to you, no one can see the kingdom of God without being born from above.' Nicodemus said to him, 'How can a person once grown old be born again? Surely he cannot reenter his mother's womb and be born again, can he?' Jesus answered, 'No one can enter the kingdom of God without being born of water and Spirit. What is born of flesh is flesh, and what is born of spirit is spirit.' " *John 3:3–6*

When Jesus spoke of being born again, perhaps he meant that if we have the Spirit, then we are always being born—born, that is, into the reality of God's own life.

Some early church writers discerned a temporal difference between our being made in the image of God and our being made in the divine likeness. At birth we are made in God's image, but it is through grace and over time that we are finally made in God's likeness. For Christ is the likeness of God, and our business is to become like Christ. We are not fully human, fully created in God's image and likeness, until we have put on the mind and heart of Christ. That is where human perfection lies.

60

It is tempting to keep looking fondly to the past and to view unrealistically the way things were. Some people imagine that the human race originated in Eden, a place of innocence and pristine beauty, where Adam and Eve issued from God's hands perfectly made. That perfection, which they compare to the innocence of a child, was lost because of the disobedience of our first parents. This loss is then sadly relived as each child reaches the age of discretion, becomes capable of doing wrong, and actually does so.

But something is missing from such a picture. For one thing, it fails to take into account that the future of the human race is not determined by its failed beginning but by its re-creation in Christ. This means, of course, that despite sin's entrance into the human story, God never abandoned us. The creation story was hardly over in the garden of Eden. God's creative action would continue throughout salvation history. Perhaps we ought to say, therefore, that the perfection we seek lies ahead of us, not behind us. To develop the insight of Irenaeus, the measure of our sinfulness should be taken, not against the background of what the human race once possessed and then lost, but in terms of the possibility for full humanity which lies ahead of us yet which feels at times so unreachable.

But there is another point. The creation account is not an historical reminiscence but a theologically motivated story. Eden never existed. It seems instead to be a dream of how things ought to have been rather than how they once were. If that is the case, then the dream of paradise points ahead of us, not to a primeval past. The image of all creatures living at peace with God and one another may have been pushed backward into the dawn of history, and the loss of that gift can only give rise to regret. In that view, human history begins on a very sorry note. But Eden may actually represent a vision of something we hope for. If so, then the longing symbolized in that scene can help to focus the future, both the future of the human race and the personal future which will be realized as each of us becomes fully the creature which God intends. To believe that God is our creator is to look to the future with confidence, because our vision has been centered on the God "who is and who was and who is to come" (Revelation 1:8).[5]

Our becoming human, then, does not end with our conception and birth. Nor are we fully and finally human when we reach seven, or sixteen, or twenty-one. From a religious point of view, becoming human means becoming free; becoming a person entails growing in our capacity for unselfish love. When is that process over? To paraphrase Irenaeus, we are not made divine at our beginning, but first we are made human and then we are made divine.[6] That is, over a lifetime we are drawn into the very life of God, sharing ever more fully in the nature of him who humbled himself to share our humanity. Obviously, this process of being made—or being redeemed, or being made holy, or divinized: it amounts to the same thing—is not going to end until we die. We are always capable of growing less selfish, more trusting and compassionate, more of a believer, less threatened and insecure, more open to the challenges and possibilities which arise from being with Christ.

Anyone who seriously believes in creation realizes that the Spirit is constantly hovering over us, creating and renewing us. Throughout our lives we respond daily to the impulse of the Spirit and to the subtle ways by which the mysteries of faith attract us to God. For the simple fact is that if people do not love, if they do not believe, if they do not face the future with hope, then they will never be humanly fulfilled. Everything in life conforms to this basic law. Everything we set ourselves to do must obey the elementary principles which St.

Ignatius Loyola summarized at the beginning of his *Spiritual Exercises* (I ask the reader to pardon the sexually exclusive language of the text):

"Man is created to praise, reverence, and serve God our Lord, and by this means to save his soul. The other things on the face of the earth are created for man to help him in attaining the end for which he is created. Hence, man is to make use of them in as far as they help him in the attainment of his end, and he must rid himself of them in as far as they prove a hindrance to him. . . . Our one desire and choice should be what is more conducive to the end for which we are created."[7]

This brief statement marks out for us the chief characteristics of our human existence. "Do you believe in God, the Father almighty, creator of heaven and earth?" The only way to answer affirmatively is by leading a life which is one continual act of praise, reverence, and service. This means observing the basic teachings of our religious tradition. It means loving God our creator and Lord above all things, and loving our neighbors as we love ourselves. It means that we praise and adore God most profoundly, not merely when we bow our heads in silent prayer, but when we try to act as children of God would act, that is, as Jesus taught us. Needless to say, we are not Jesus and we are not living in first-century Palestine. We have to translate the gospel message within the framework of the late twentieth century. What following Jesus means concretely for each of us is something to be prayed over and carefully discerned. But discipleship certainly demands as much now as it did among Jesus' first followers.

The reverence which we show toward God in our private or in our communal worship should carry over into daily life. Do we treat other men and women with reverence, acknowledging by the way we speak to them or about them that they too are being created and loved by God? Do we treat the earth reverently, like stewards to whom much has been entrusted? Or do we waste energy, food, and water, oblivious to those in the world less fortunate than we? Have we forgotten that the earth was created by God and that our residing here can only be temporary? Are we attached to material things and do we acquire possessions whether we need them or not? Are we ready to share our goods? Do we ever wonder how God regards us when wealthy countries, like ours, turn so much of their creative energies and material resources into developing weapons of annihilation? Is this a reverent use of the earth's riches?

The fact that we are creatures places no limitations upon our creativity and freedom, as if the praise and obedience we owe to God in some way diminishes our humanity. The truth lies in exactly the opposite direction. Serving and obeying God, that is, paying close attention to the word of God and keeping it (Luke 11:28), is the only way to real human liberation. God is no tyrant. Realizing that we are creatures does force us, however, to meditate on our radical dependence upon God even as we use the powerful desires, drives, and creative energies which God has placed within us.

Many people are drawn to reflect upon the Psalms because they find such rugged reassurance in those ancient prayers. The Psalms speak of wonder, of beauty, of mystery, and of creation as gift. They complain to God about wickedness in the world, and remind God that things are not well when evil people prosper and the fortunes of good people fail. The mouth of the psalmist has tasted guilt and sin, and God's soul-parching silence. All of these sentiments figure into the making of the human spirit. In the Psalms life's inner reality advances to the fore in a moment of prayer or intense spiritual insight, and often after praying them even the most intractable problems feel uncomplicated and bearable. For some people, these moments of praise and thanksgiving, of desperate hope and repentance, expand into a complete lifestyle which views every experience in terms of God's ongoing creation. For such people, God is truly "creator of heaven and earth."

TO BELIEVE IN THE MYSTERY OF GOD

The Church asks us, "Do you believe in God, the Father Almighty, creator of heaven and earth?" We have been reflecting on the various elements of this question, yet perhaps now we should step back from the parts and ask ourselves whether, finally, we are ready to live with the mystery of God. Recall the transfiguration story. After the event on the mountain, the disciples resumed their life with Jesus. The weight and routine of the familiar gradually resumed. The memory of the transfiguration apparently did not keep them awake when Jesus went to pray in the garden on the night he was betrayed. The mystery had been revealed, but were they prepared to live with it? They heard the voice, but were they ready really to listen to Jesus?

The Christian notion of God, the baptismal profession seems to be suggesting, consists of two elements: God is creator and God is Father. We might add that God is also mystery, silent and incomprehensible, immanent within human hearts and at the same time utterly transcendent. God is the inner space against which all human thinking, deciding, acting, loving, and desiring take place. Without that space human beings would collapse into one-dimensional flatness, and yet that space itself is never to be seen, never to be conceptualized.

The divine mystery appears breathtakingly close. The human heart reaches out to it, desperately seeking love, forgiveness, communion, and life. It is so close, in fact, that its presence sometimes feels indistinguishable from a sense of its absence. Some have described that mystery as power itself, or goodness, or beauty, or truth itself. Yet these descriptions will probably sound like empty abstractions to those who have honestly and humbly called to God from the quiet depths of their hearts. On the one hand, the divine reality breaks into our lives like a voice from a cloud—like a presence which is always there but never visible. Yet on the other hand, this mystery is passionately involved with human beings, drawing them to itself as firmly and tenderly as a mother or father caressing an infant. Jesus addressed this otherwise nameless mystery "Father." For him, trusting surrender was the only conceivable response to the holy mystery of God. Until one has surrendered to that presence, totally and unreservedly, fully human life will not have begun and the word "God" will remain indecipherable.

It is easy to take the teachings of our faith for granted. Doctrinal formulas are effortlessly repeated. Though we would never think of denying them, they can easily lose their power to revolutionize the way we live. I am not sure why this happens, but many of us can testify about how quickly the reality of God fades from view when we cease looking for God.

Some Christians have simply given up wrestling with the mystery of God. They are not sure whether they made the right choice regarding the overall direction of their lives, but they realize that now it is too late to reverse things and start over. Lifelong questions about the meaning and goal of human existence remain unanswered; faith in God has never been confirmed by definitive, unambiguous experiences of God. Were the events or circumstances in which they thought God had a hand really signs of God's presence, or were they simply neutral occurrences which could have been interpreted either in terms of God or apart from God? They have lost the energy to think about such things any more, or to continue wrestling with God. They continue to pray, hoping that there is a God who listens; but they cannot be sure. They continue to lead morally righteous lives because they are Christian more or less by habit. Yet the general tone which pervades their religious life becomes one of passive resignation. They are believing on a wager: in the long run one should bank on the reality of God. But in the short run this only yields a certain sadness of soul. They go about the practice of their religion like someone reluctantly paying premiums on an insurance policy. Life feels inconclusive. Perhaps this happens because at some point in their lives they determined, more or less consciously, to keep the mystery of God at a distance. They may have realized that taking the reality of God seriously would cost more than they were prepared to spend.

There are also some Christians who never exactly gave up their search for God, yet they never felt comfortable in God's presence, either. They tried to think of God and to pray but, after a few moments, they did not know what to say. The ensuing silence made them restless and they would start to think of the many things which needed to be done. They persuaded themselves that they would profit more by throwing themselves into their work, or helping their neighbor, or doing something extra for their families, or if they were clerics, by hearing a confession, or visiting the sick, or counseling someone in distress. They would welcome any diversion from the unsettling silence of being in God's presence and not knowing what to do or say next. Afterwards they felt a bit guilty. But, then, was God not at least partly responsible? Could God not have broken through the unbearable quiet? Why not a transfiguration experience that would shatter all doubts? These people are not sure how to answer. Yet one thing seems clear. They too eventually surrendered on life rather than struggle with the silence of the divine mystery.

Finally, there are Christians who have neither resigned from the struggle nor chosen to avoid it. They have experienced God as the one who liberates them from their fears and insecurities. God empowers them to take risks, to dare to believe and to hope even while many men and women, some of them family and close friends, have drifted away from religious belief. They have experienced God. Their imaginations are engaged by the possibilities Jesus envisioned when he preached about the kingdom. The mystery of God is at the root of every lifegiving challenge they face, and they take time to be present to that mystery, to contemplate it. They do so because they must. They want to be wherever God is, and since they cannot pin God down in any one place, or in any one idea, they experience life as pilgrims. Their interior life is full of movement. Such people are on fire with love, and because God is love, they feel themselves to be drawn inescapably into the depths of that mystery. Such people are not exempt from the demands and frustrations of ordinary living; far from it. But for them the ordinary does not turn into an unappetizing dullness; frustrations do not turn them into people who wander through life passively and sadly. God is ever the creator and in their living they experience God's creative action. To put matters simply, they are men and women alive, and they exist this way because they would not run away from the mystery of God. Perhaps the question we continually need to ask is whether we really want to allow this mystery into our lives. Perhaps this too should be part of our baptismal renewal.

NOTES

1. See Joseph A. Fitzmyer, *The Gospel According to Luke I–IX* (New York: Doubleday & Co., 2nd edition, 1983), pp. 791–797.

2. The significance of Jesus' *Abba* experience has been studied and developed by many writers. Several recent contributions are: Bernard Cooke, "Non-Patriarchal Salvation," in *Women's Spirituality: Resources for Christian Development*, ed. Joann Wolski Conn (Mahwah, N.J.: Paulist Press, 1986), pp. 274–286; Eamonn Bredin, *Rediscovering Jesus: Challenge of Discipleship* (Mystic, Conn.: Twenty-Third Publications, 1985); and James Dunn, *Jesus and the Spirit* (Philadelphia: Westminster Press, 1975), pp. 11–92.

3. Hans Urs von Balthasar, *Origen: Spirit and Fire: A Thematic Anthology of His Writings*, trans. Robert J. Daly (Washington, D.C.: Catholic University of America Press, 1984), p. 122.

4. Henry Bettenson, ed., *The Early Christian Fathers* (Oxford: Oxford University Press, 1978 [fourth impression]), pp. 67–68. Emphasis added.

5. Edward Schillebeexck writes: "Creation is a blank cheque to which only God himself stands guarantor. It is a vote of confidence which gives the person who believes in the creator God the courage to believe in word and deed that the kingdom of God, i.e. truly human salvation, well-being and happiness, despite many experiences of disaster, is in fact in the making for humanity, in the power of God's creation which summons men and women to realize it. Therefore, God, the one who may be trusted, is, in all his absolute divine freedom, a constant surprise for humanity: 'He is the one who was and is to come' (Rev. 1:8, 4:8)" (*On Christian Faith*, trans. John Bowden [New York: Crossroad Publishing Co., 1987], p. 18).

6. Bettenson, *The Early Christian Fathers*, p. 69.

7. *The Spiritual Exercises of St. Ignatius*, trans. Louis J. Puhl, S.J. (Chicago: Loyola University Press, 1951), p. 12.

Chapter Three

Do You Believe in Jesus Christ?

Philosophers have measured mountains
Fathomed the depths of seas, of states, and kings,
Walked with a staff to heav'n, and traced fountains:

But there are two vast, spacious things,
The which to measure it doth more behove:
Yet few there are that sound them; Sin and Love.

George Herbert

The second question of the baptismal profession of
faith asks, "Do you believe in Jesus Christ, his only
Son, our Lord, who was born of the Virgin Mary, was
crucified, died, and was buried, rose from the dead,
and is now seated at the right hand of the Father?"
Without doubt, the central doctrine of Christian faith is
our belief in Jesus Christ. No doubt, too, that if someone were to inquire of us what we believe about Jesus,
most of us would answer that he is God's Son, that he
is divine while sharing our human nature, that he suffered and died to save us from our sins, and that he
has been raised from the dead. While he lived among
us, we might continue, Jesus chose certain people to be
his followers. He taught them about God and how to
live together as brothers and sisters, and he commis-
sioned them to carry on his work after his death, pri-
marily by preaching the gospel and establishing the
Church.

On the purely historical level, we know that Jesus was

born, and that he was crucified, died, and was buried. But these historical events carry enormous religious significance when viewed in the light of faith. Hence the Church confesses that Jesus is the Lord, God's Son, raised from the dead, who now lives with the Father in glory. What makes those historical events significant is that we are talking about the birth, crucifixion, death, and burial of *Jesus;* and what makes the life of Jesus significant is that God raised him from the dead. Without resurrection, Jesus would have been forgotten as one more itinerant preacher. Without Easter, the disciples would not have been led to call him Lord, nor would any community have declared him the Son of God or the Word made flesh.

DO YOU BELIEVE IN JESUS CHRIST, HIS ONLY SON, OUR LORD?

If Jesus Christ is divine, as the Church professes, then it makes perfect sense for men and women to place their trust in him and obey his teaching. But how did we arrive at the conclusion that Jesus is God's Son? We accepted this belief because we have been reared as Christians (at least, most of us have). Our parents or others have taught us about Jesus and we have assented to their belief about him; that is, we have accepted the faith of the Church. Some people slide into their Christianness; it never occurred to them to doubt the teaching of the Church or the belief of their families and friends. Some have passed through periods of questioning. They may even have ceased practicing their faith, as we often say, for a number of years. Eventually, however, they have a change of heart, either because they have recovered something true and lifegiving in Christian faith, or else simply because of the inertial force of their upbringing. Others may never return to the Church. Perhaps they have found God elsewhere, or they have simply renounced belief in

God altogether, or, like the seed that fell among the rocks and thorns, whatever faith they once possessed withered through sin or was choked by the cares and attractions of the world. Still others wrestle for a long time with the mystery of God and endeavor their whole lives to remain faithful to the gospel. In one way or another, they have found Jesus. Wherever men and women come to believe in Jesus Christ, there the Spirit of God has been at work in their minds and hearts.

Most of us would readily agree that our belief in Jesus ought to be far more than a matter of correct ideas about him and knowing the facts about his earthly life. Anyone can repeat the phrases "was born of the Virgin Mary, was crucified, died, and was buried." Anyone can say "Lord, Lord." But that may signify nothing more than that we know his correct title, as Jesus himself said: "Not everyone who says to me, 'Lord, Lord,' will enter the kingdom of heaven, but only the one who does the will of my Father in heaven" (Matthew 7:21). Even the demons acknowledged that Jesus was the Son of the Most High God (e.g., Mark 5:7 or Luke 4:34). The one who really believes in Jesus proves this by the way he or she lives. But why, finally, do we believe? Because someone has told us about Jesus? Do we believe on the basis of someone else's faith? Or do we believe in Jesus because, after following him for a while, we have found him to be the one who satisfies our heart's desire? Do we believe in him because we have discovered his teaching and example to be infinitely attractive? Have we found in his humanness the ideal self which we hope someday will be ours? Has Jesus become for us more than a set of doctrines and ethical principles, has he himself become the way, the truth, and the life for us?

Ultimately, the logic of faith has to be the logic of love. We love, and therefore we follow. We love, and therefore we believe.

There is no great mystery as to why we happen to be Christians, but there can be a great deal of mystery involved in why we remain such. Most of us are Christian because we were born and raised in Christian families. Our reason for staying Christian, however, must go beyond this. And that is why I say that faith, finally, obeys the logic of love. As mature Christians, we believe in Jesus because we love him, not out of some childish attachment or adolescent sentimentality, but with the freedom, courage, and depth of adult love. We live according to his teaching because, finally, love measures everything. Love determines how much of ourselves we are willing to give, how much we are willing to surrender, how much self-emptying we are ready to undergo. "If you keep my commandments, you will remain in my love" (John 15:10). I do not think Jesus means, "I will love you only if you obey me." That would border on manipulating people into remaining loyal to him. The sense would seem to be: "If you realize how deeply I have loved you, then you will have no hesitation about doing what I ask." For he also says, "Whoever has my commandments and observes them is the one who loves me" (John 14:21), and "Whoever loves me will keep my word" (John 14:23). Love confirms itself through doing what Jesus asks, and the fact that his followers do what Jesus asks proves that they are living out of love for him. When the Church questions us as to whether we believe in Jesus Christ, therefore, it is aware that faith in Jesus which is not at the same time love for him is meaningless. And love proves itself in deeds, not in words.

From time to time people ask about particular Catholic practices, such as whether it is still a sin to miss Mass on Sunday. Generally I answer that they may be posing the wrong question. Indeed, because faith is God's gift—as is human life itself—we have the responsibility of nurturing and protecting it; the failure to do so would be wrong. An important way of both expressing and protecting our faith is through the Sunday Eucharist with a believing community. But the more fundamental question is, Does anyone have to be or to remain Christian? I phrase it this way in order to emphasize the point that being Christian must eventually be the result of a choice. Being Christian is a matter of freedom. One freely chooses to follow Jesus. One may also freely choose not to follow Jesus, although the reasons for deciding not to follow him usually have less to do with Jesus than with poor preaching and catechesis about him, or the sorry example of those who profess to be Christian, or a person's unwillingness to be challenged by the gospel and to break away from a sinful way of life.

Nevertheless, no one has to be Christian, or Catholic. Until we have come to terms with that, then questions about specific Christian practices make little sense. Being Christian means thinking with the mind and heart of Christ; it means discipleship. It also means living the same faith with other men and women, and together with them praising and worshiping God in Christ. Perhaps we take our first step in this direction when we start envisioning ourselves standing with the disciples as Jesus asked, "What are you looking for?" (John 1:38) That is the question we need to keep hearing. For we have to make up our minds, freely and deliberately, that God is what we are looking for and Jesus is our way.

Unless love springs from freedom it is not genuine. We cannot be forced into loving someone, not even into loving God. We can be coerced into obedience and conformity, but not into love. If Jesus was not free, then his commitment to doing the Father's will becomes meaningless. And if we are not free, then our religious and moral practice is nothing but empty gesture. It is unlikely, however, that freedom is an all-or-nothing proposition; we are free (or unfree) to a greater or lesser extent. Which means that our religious and moral activity can be more or less alive, depending upon how deeply we have really loved God.

Who is this person, Jesus Christ, God's only Son and our Lord? Perhaps we can answer this in terms of the gospel reading for the Third Sunday of Lent, in the A cycle. Jesus is the Messiah, the Anointed One of God, as the woman at the well said (John 4:25). Jesus is the Christ, the one whom the Father has anointed with the Spirit. He is the one sent by the Father to reconcile those estranged from God and their fellow human beings, whether they are Jews, or Samaritans, or anyone else. This Jesus is the living water who satisfies the human thirst for acceptance and for freedom: "Whoever drinks the water I shall give will never thirst" (John 4:14). Jesus Christ is God's answer to humanity's most profound longing, that is, its longing for communion with God and for union among men and women. He is the one through whom God gives the Spirit, the gift which is destined for the whole human race, not just for one people or one race: "But the hour is coming, and is now here, when true worshipers will worship the Father in Spirit and truth; and indeed, the Father seeks such people to worship him" (John 4:23). Jesus is the Son whose entire being was for the Father: "My food is to do the will of the one who sent me and to finish his work" (John 4:34). In Jesus the Father's compassion and forgiveness have been revealed.

WHO WAS BORN OF THE VIRGIN MARY

This statement of belief draws our attention to three things. First, like us Jesus is a fully human being. He was born into a particular people, at a certain place and time, with inherited physical characteristics, just as we are. As Paul wrote, "But when the fullness of time had come, God sent his Son, born of a woman, born under

75

the law . . ." (Galatians 4:4). He was born into a human family where he learned how to walk and to speak, to read and to relate to others, to work and to pray, and so forth. He grew physically, psychologically, and religiously, advancing in "wisdom and age and favor before God and man" (Luke 2:52).

Secondly, we believe that he was born of the Virgin Mary. The Church's belief about Mary's virginity underlines what we believe about Jesus. His true Father was God, which means that he is God's Son and therefore is fully divine, while as Mary's son he is fully human. By recalling the fact that Jesus was born into the world as we are, the Church is emphasizing that Jesus is fully human. Yet at the same time it is safeguarding the truth that he is also different from us. Jesus was one with God in a way that we are not. When Jesus called God his Father, he spoke the literal truth.

Thirdly, the figure of Mary is always linked to Jesus; she cannot be understood apart from him. Because Jesus was her son, Mary has been drawn prominently into the history of salvation. Wherever she is venerated, as Vatican II teaches, she necessarily leads people closer to Christ [The Dogmatic Constitution on the Church, #65]. Such is her role in the history and life of the Church. Her faith to some degree becomes our faith, as John Paul II has written:

"Mary's faith, according to the Church's apostolic witness, in some way continues to become the faith of the pilgrim people of God: the faith of individuals and communities, of places and gatherings, and of the various groups existing in the Church. It is a faith that is passed on simultaneously through both the mind and the heart." *Redemptoris Mater*, #28

This means that, above all, Mary is mentioned in the creed—and in the baptismal profession of faith—because she was a believer: "Blessed are you who *be-*

lieved" (Luke 1:45). Of the many things which can be said of her, this has to be first. Mary believed. She trusted. She stood next to Jesus as he died on the cross. Mary follows Jesus in the creed because she followed him in faith.

THE HUMANNESS OF JESUS

In recent years there has been a great deal of writing about Jesus. Theologians and scripture scholars have been studying the gospels in order to shed as much light as possible on the humanness of Jesus. They have been engaged in a considerable amount of research into the social, historical, and cultural background of the New Testament writings. The gospels, they tell us, do provide some information about Jesus' career. The gospels are, in a very broad sense, historical, although it was not the intention of the evangelists simply to compose biographical accounts of the life of Jesus. Actually, the gospels supply considerable information about the life of some early Christian communities that were trying to live the way Jesus had taught. They have a great deal to say about the problems, the struggles, the controversies and achievements of the early church.[1]

Essentially the gospels are faith documents, written by believers for believers. The gospels are not simply stories about Jesus. They are stories about people who came to believe in him, about his effect on their lives, about a distinctively new experience of God. The gospels are not so much lives of Jesus as stories of Jesus' life in and through the first few generations of Christians. They are, in other words, stories of Jesus' life in us and among us. The early Christians could not tell about Jesus without talking about themselves; and the same thing holds true today. As we tell the story of our lives, to the degree that we really believe in Jesus, we are at the same time telling the story of his life.

While Scripture is the important source for our knowledge of Jesus, early Christian writers (the Church Fathers) devoted great attention to the person of Christ, and we are privileged to have much of their work. They did not improve upon the New Testament writings, but they looked deeply into what these writings were telling the believing community of a later age. Succeeding generations would raise questions about Jesus which had not been envisioned by the evangelists, or a thinker and apostle like Paul. It was the Christian writers of the first five centuries who drew out some implications of the New Testament material. They also formulated the Church's faith in doctrinal language, which found its way into the creeds and the professions of faith, like our present baptismal promises. Jesus Christ, they confessed, was truly God and truly human; that was the heart of Christian belief.

Yet, having affirmed that Jesus is truly divine, we have to be careful that we do not dismiss anything else which could be said about Jesus as of secondary importance. The Jesus of the gospel stories must not be swamped by our belief in his divinity; otherwise his humanity will appear less and less meaningful. When such imbalance occurs, our appreciation of our own humanness will be diminished, since Jesus' story must somehow also be ours. To lose sight of his humanity is to lose sight of our own. Since we do not have a divine nature, nothing in us would correspond to what is so special and distinctive about Jesus. The story of salvation would then become exclusively Jesus' thing. It would become the story of what God has done for us, whether people ever heard about Jesus or not.

What a number of modern theologians have been attempting, then, employing many of the literary and historical insights won from modern biblical scholarship, is a recovery of Jesus' humanity. They have made us aware of the necessary balance between Jesus' humanity and his divinity.[2] The first disciples gradually comprehended who Jesus was without ever thinking about a distinction between divine and human natures in him. They just knew Jesus as a human being, a man, a carpenter's son from Galilee. They lived with him, they ate and drank with him, they watched him teach, and heal, and forgive sins. They were his companions when he traveled up and down Palestine, and they talked often with Jesus about the reign of God in the world. Those disciples knew Jesus, not with the technical theology of later doctrinal formulas, but with the lived, experiential knowledge that comes from being in the company of someone they had grown to trust and to love.

First and foremost, therefore, Jesus was for them a human being who had given himself totally to the mystery of God. They saw that Jesus really believed that God was his Father, and in some profound way which they would never be able to explain satisfactorily (any more than the later church could), they realized that this was in fact the case. From then on, God for them would be the one who was Father for Jesus. In short, when the disciples accepted Jesus as their teacher and, after the resurrection, as their Lord, they also accepted Jesus' faith. Jesus was a believer too. There would have been no chance of following him if Jesus were not human as they were. Discipleship would have been impossible if Jesus had such an advantage over us that he never fully shared our condition.

Unless Jesus were completely human, all that he did would have been bloodless. There would have been no real struggle, no real testing, no real tears, no real hunger and thirst, no real feelings of abandonment or loneliness, no real sorrow when someone close to him died, no need to pray or to think, no heartaches, no real outrage over injustice or hypocrisy. How in the world would Jesus matter to us if he had not been fully a part of the human condition? How could we ever relate to him? If Jesus were not completely human, then whenever he urged his disciples to forgive, or to sell their possessions and give to the poor, or to pray for their enemies, the disciple could rightfully have rejoined that such behavior was easy for Jesus because he, after all, had the advantage of divinity. He could work miracles. He could count on God to send angels to defend him. He had no family to support, and so he could go to prison if he had to, without worrying about a wife and children. And finally, he would never have to be anxious about the future because, being divine, he already knew what was going to happen.

False conceptions about Jesus' divinity completely wipe out the possibility of Jesus' having a credible human story. It does not help matters to say that, being divine, he felt things all the more intensely. Being sensitive and experiencing life deeply and intensely are not divine qualities; they are qualities of a humanity which has not been compromised by sin and guilt. To believe in Jesus, then, is to believe that human nature—the humanity which Jesus and we together share—is our route to God. For us there is no bypassing the burden and challenge which being human imposes upon us, any more than Jesus could have bypassed it.

WHO WAS CRUCIFIED, DIED, AND WAS BURIED

Once again history and theology intersect, for these three events underline the fact that Jesus, God's anointed, really suffered; he was really put to death; and he was really buried in the earth. He experienced death, not as the natural end of human life, but as the result of betrayal and profound injustice. Although he was delivered up by his own people, he was sentenced and executed by the Romans—by the gentiles—in a form of punishment reserved for slaves. These historical facts underline the real humanity of Jesus. There was no pretending, no last minute escape, no choirs of angels to soften the humiliation, the agony, or the experience of abandonment.

The natural question which these events raise for us is, Why did all this happen? Jesus himself answered it: "for the forgiveness of sins" (Matthew 26:28). Jesus' suffering and death on the cross is so tied up with the mystery of sin, repentance, and forgiveness, that we cannot discuss the one apart from the other. In this section there are four ideas to consider. First, we should think about why Jesus is so concerned about sinners. Next we need to recall who Jesus is, precisely because he is the one who assures us of God's forgiveness. Then we want to reflect on whether we clearly appreciate our need for repentance and forgiveness, since without such an awareness we will not understand what Jesus did for us. Finally, we face the fact that Jesus died so that our sins might be forgiven.

The other gospel texts for the Third Sunday of Lent may help to center our reflection here. In John 2:13–25, we hear how Jesus clears the temple of merchants and money-changers; and in Luke 13:1–9, we listen to the passage about repentance and a barren fig tree. Both of these readings relate to the theme of repentance and conversion.

The temple was the place where one would expect to find holiness, but instead the buyers and sellers, and the money-changers have profaned the sacred place. Rather than finding people behaving righteously and humbly in God's presence, Jesus finds his Father's house desecrated, and he clears it. When the Lord comes to us, what will he find? Will he find our hearts and minds to be the dwelling place of the Spirit, or will he find them cluttered, profaned, and disoriented?

In Luke 13:1–9, Jesus is informed by some people of the Galilean pilgrims to the temple whom Pilate had slaughtered. Jesus in turn reminds them of a second incident when eighteen innocent people were killed by a falling tower. These victims, Jesus says, had not suffered because they were worse sinners than everybody else. Twice he insists, "But I tell you, if you do not repent, you will all perish as they did" (Luke 13:3, 5). The point Jesus seems to be drawing is that death can come suddenly to anyone, and therefore, the moment for change of heart is now. This episode is followed by a parable about a barren fig tree, which is likewise about repentance. Unless we start to bear fruit, then we too shall be cut down.

1. Jesus' concern for the sinner
Throughout the gospels, Jesus insists upon repentance. He repeatedly calls men and women to reverse the direction of their living by changing their hearts. Jesus was not simply a prophet like John the Baptist preaching and encouraging moral reform. He did not campaign against sin the way John did. He did not shout, "You brood of vipers! Who warned you to flee from the coming wrath?" (Matthew 3:7) Jesus would not break the bruised reed, nor would he quench the smoldering wick (Matthew 12:20). Jesus was not a moral zealot, advocating ethical righteousness for its own sake. On the one hand, Jesus wanted his followers to exceed the scribes and the Pharisees in their practice of virtue (Matthew 5:20). Yet, on the other hand, literal observance of moral or religious precepts did not mean that a person automatically knew and experienced divine acceptance. There could be no righteousness before God apart from faith.

In short, Jesus' call to repentance went far beyond any concern with virtue for its own sake. Rather, Jesus preached repentance because he loved people. He loved them both for what they were and for what they could be. When human beings are locked inside themselves, prisoners to sin, they are not free. They are not experiencing life as daughters and sons of God. Surely, sometimes people must have frustrated him because of their blindness and their resistance to change. New wine would demand new wineskins (Mark 2:22). The worst cases must have been those who believed they were leading decent lives and therefore presumed that Jesus' call for change of heart could not be directed at them. After all, what things did they have to change? What things were they doing which demanded repentance? Apart from the small human failings to which all men and women are prone, even the most religious among us, what was so desperately wrong with their lives? Why did Jesus keep teaching that *all* must repent, or perish?

People who felt this way disturbed him deeply. They included those whose lives were softened by wealth, those who had powerful political and religious connections which they dared not offend, and those who had lost their integrity but paraded before God as if they had not. They included people like the lawyers and the scribes who, instead of contemplating the mystery of God, tried to master it. They were people who had no trouble finding God in their families and friends, but refused to try to look for God in strangers and outsiders, or who regularly attended church but never visited someone in prison or in a hospital, or who mouthed prayers of thanksgiving while feeling they had a right to what they enjoyed because they had worked for it. They were men and women who let others borrow things but kept chafing until their goods were returned, or who could not abide others more virtuous, more prosperous, or better educated than they, and yet took no steps to improve. They were people who complained about doing things for show but never ceased judging the intentions of others, or who refused to forget insults or injuries, or who were threatened by other people's successes, or talent, or innocence. All these types illustrated the sorry state of human freedom as Jesus encountered it, the ways in which human beings had lost the spontaneity which comes from being children of God.

These are the kinds of things the "ordinary sinner" must contend with. Jesus was not just trying to correct all forms of human shortsightedness through his teaching and example. Above all, he was concerned that men and women open themselves to letting God reign in their minds and hearts. He was drawing people to the kingdom of God: to think the kingdom, to breathe the kingdom, to imagine and to dream it, to live the kingdom from day to day. But human sinfulness kept blocking their awareness, their ability to hear what he was talking about. They had eyes but could not see, and ears but could not hear. Jesus' major concern was that people should know and love God. What characterizes every manifestation of human sinfulness is the persistent preoccupation with oneself. Sin traps people within themselves, inside their prejudices and routines, and their infinite capacities for self-justification. This is not the way God intended human beings to be, and Jesus knew it. But how to get people to change? How to bring people to mend their ways? How to help people to acknowledge their blindness? For this we need God's grace; for this we need a savior.

2. Who is Jesus?
This question sounds so simple, but it may not be easy to answer. The language of the creed, for instance, is simple and direct, but it is not immediately clear to many people what the Church means when it speaks of Jesus as "one in being with the Father." To confess that Jesus is "true God and true man" needs spelling out. The only example of being human and divine that we have is Jesus, and the first thing we have to say is

84

that the disciples encountered him as a man, not as a god.

In order to "explain" the person of Jesus, the Church distinguished two natures in him. Yet no matter how carefully one presents the theory about two natures in one person, it still seems to some people that there were two persons or two selves inside of Jesus. Or they seem to think that basically Jesus was God but that he had temporarily surrendered or concealed his divine powers. Why then does the gospel story highlight Jesus' powerlessness and his poverty, his humility and his obedience? Are these human qualities or divine qualities? Has not Jesus given us a very different picture of what being God-like means? Does not the mystery of power being made perfect in weakness enable us to glimpse something startlingly different about God? In other words, has not the death of Jesus on the cross revolutionized the way we understand divinity? It goes without saying that unless Jesus was God's Son, his living and his dying would not have been all that remarkable. But because of his oneness with the Father, the life and death of Jesus redefine for us not only the meaning of divinity but also what it means to be human. Jesus is both God's way of being human and the human expression of being divine.

What do we say then? With the gospel writers at least we can maintain that Jesus was filled with the Holy Spirit, that he came from God, that God loved him as a son, and that he believed God was his Father. Or, as Paul phrased it, "For in him all the fullness [of God] was pleased to dwell" (Colossians 1:19). The Church would never have reached this level of belief if the first disciples had not experienced Jesus raised from the dead. Resurrection faith gave rise to the Church's belief in the divinity of Christ. Without Easter there would have been no ongoing reflection on the person and significance of Jesus. And resurrection faith continues to give rise to the Church's belief in the Lordship of Christ. For the fact is that Christians still experience Jesus in their midst.

Each of us could report his or her own evidence for Jesus, what he means for us, how we believe we have experienced his presence in our lives, and so forth. Each of us probably cherishes a favorite image of Jesus, a particularly moving gospel story or scene, or some few moments in our lives when Jesus seemed extremely caring and close to us. Each of us knows something about him which cannot be satisfactorily put into words. We grasp intuitively something of the mystery of God which has become present to us in and through Jesus, when, for instance, we hold a crucifix in our hands, or devoutly kneel before the tabernacle, or see the face of someone who is very poor. We sense the presence in our lives of some power which is attracting us to live more authentically, which enables us to trust and to love, which accepts us at the same time it challenges us to mend our ways. What we are sensing in various ways is the power of the Spirit who makes Jesus really and personally present among us.

Jesus, we believe, came from God. This is not to suggest that Jesus literally descended to the earth from some other world. To say "Jesus came down from heaven," as the creed does, is to speak in images. Heaven is not literally up above, and Jesus' descent or coming down is not to be interpreted spatially. Like us, Jesus was born into human history, and whoever is born into human history comes from God, since God is our creator. But since we are always in the process of being created, we can say that Jesus was continually coming from God. Each day of his life he was being sent into the world as someone who was thoroughly a part of human history. Jesus was born of a particular people, with a definite bloodline and physical traits; he was born into a culture and society, just as we are. He learned to see and describe the world from a limited standpoint, just as we do. Jesus' entire life was mission. He knew himself to be one whom God had sent, and was daily sending, to preach the good news about God's kingdom.

Since Jesus is human, most of the things which can be said about him likewise apply to us. We also come from God and are sent into the world, to carry on Jesus' work of announcing the kingdom. Of course, we would not be thinking or talking about being sent to carry out Jesus' work if we had not inherited Christian faith. That faith has shaped our outlook on the world and on ourselves. Jesus' way has come to feel right to us, almost natural, and certainly reasonable, even when following Jesus entails struggle. Yet he is different from us too, although we may be at a loss to explain what this difference consists of. Maybe we can only reaffirm that without Jesus we would not know and experience God the way we do. For our sake, God sent Jesus as the beloved Son, the first-born among many brothers and sisters. Without Jesus we would never have guessed the great calling which is ours, namely:

". . . that Christ may dwell in your hearts through faith; that you, rooted and grounded in love, may have strength to comprehend with all the holy ones what is the breadth and length and height and depth, and to know the love of Christ that surpasses all knowledge, *so that you may be filled with all the fullness of God.*" *Ephesians 3:17–19*

The point bears repeating. To be filled to the measure of our capacity with the "fullness of God" is to share that very fullness which dwelled in Jesus completely and made him God's Son.

Whatever the Church believes about Jesus derives from the way his disciples experienced him, and, we should add, from the way those who follow Jesus continue to experience him. The Church grasps who Jesus is on the basis of what he does, and what he does is forgive sins.

The logic behind the Church's faith runs like this: the one who brings salvation, who rescues us from the power of sin, who liberates and redeems, who ransoms us from captivity, who frees us from the prison of moral and religious blindness, *that person* must be of God. Not only does Jesus announce that God forgives. Jesus also makes that forgiveness real; he actually does forgive, liberate, and heal as God does. Since God is so present in Jesus as to be one with him, Jesus must be related to God in a special way. His self, his very being, is one with God in a union so profound that we need special language to express it.[3]

3. Who are we?

There are Christians who do not have a heartfelt grasp of their need for forgiveness, and thus they never really understand Jesus. This happens, not because they cannot comprehend the language about salvation, but because—and here is something quite astonishing—they do not regard themselves as sinners, at least not in the way the gospel understands human sinfulness. Like most people, they readily admit that they have committed sins and have done things for which they are sorry. But such actions seem extrinsic to their inner selves. They do not associate sinfulness with who they are most deeply as persons. They make mistakes, but they do not view themselves as radically unfinished and in need of redemption. They might relate to Jesus as one like themselves though more gifted, or more clear-sighted, or more self-assured, or more God-centered. They may acknowledge that he is God's Son, but they know only *that* this makes him different, not *why* he is different. But so long as people have not fully realized their brokenness, their incompleteness, and their inner poverty, then the linchpin of Christian faith—that Jesus has done something for us which we are unable to do for ourselves—will not enter their experience.

Titles such as redeemer, savior, liberator, or deliverer might not be especially illuminating for some people today. Perhaps we need to be searching for other terms to describe Jesus. Yet whatever titles we adopt, the point is not to have people blaming themselves for failing to understand who Jesus is. They may have been instructed by the Church what they ought to believe, but they might not have had an opportunity to appropriate that teaching by walking the way of discipleship with men and women who knew and loved Jesus intimately. Like the Ethiopian eunuch, they need someone like the deacon Philip to sit with them and explain the good news about Jesus:

"The Spirit said to Philip, 'Go and join up with that chariot.' So Philip ran up and heard him reading Isaiah the prophet and said, 'Do you understand what you are reading?' He replied, 'How can I, unless someone instructs me?' So he invited Philip to get in and sit with him. . . . Then Philip opened his mouth and, beginning with this scripture passage, he proclaimed Jesus to him."*Acts 8:29–31, 35*

The gospel text for the Fourth Sunday of Lent (in the C cycle) is one of the New Testament's great forgiveness stories, the story of the prodigal son (Luke 15:1–3, 11–32). Jesus was not addressing himself there to runaway children, or to the tax collectors and prostitutes who often crowded around him. Luke writes:

"The tax collectors and sinners were all drawing near to listen to him, but the Pharisees and scribes began to complain, saying, 'This man welcomes sinners and eats with them.' So to them he addressed this parable." *Luke 15:1–3*

Jesus was telling his story to the righteous, to the Pharisees and the teachers of the law, to those who claimed
to see but whose inner vision was blind to what the
reign of God in human hearts means. "While he was a
long way off, his father caught sight of him, and was
filled with compassion for him. He ran to his son, embraced him and kissed him" (Luke 15:20). If the father
here represents God as Jesus knows and experiences
God, then this God is always seeing us "a long way
off." This God is "filled with compassion"; this God
even runs to meet us and to greet us with a kiss.

Yet even with such a powerful and moving story, Jesus
could not bring those who needed so much to repent
and be forgiven to be touched by the mystery of divine
forgiveness. And this, perhaps, sums up his life by the
night of the Last Supper. How was he to break through
the screen of the human refusal, not so much to accept
God's forgiveness, but to extend forgiveness to others?
God's forgiveness, after all, is gift; who would not accept it? Yet, insecure as we are, there are those who do
not want others to enjoy it too quickly, without having
earned it. They do not want those unlicensed to speak
in God's name to assure others of divine mercy, which
was why the Pharisees objected to Jesus' telling people
that their sins were forgiven.

But Jesus knew that God's forgiving us and our forgiving one another are intimately connected. Our reluctance to forgive each other closes us to receiving God's
forgiveness. It means that we never grasped what forgiveness is all about. How will human beings learn to
forgive each other? How will they help to lift the burdens of guilt, of collapsed dreams, of personal failure,
off one another's shoulders? How will they learn to let
go of resentment, and anger, and insecurity, and pride,
and selfishness in order to treat others as truly their
sisters and brothers? How will they allow God to set
them free by making up their minds that, yes, they

sorely need to declare their emptiness and their poverty before God, like the younger son in the story:

"Coming to his senses, he thought, '. . . I shall get up and go to my father and I shall say to him, Father, I have sinned against heaven and against you. I no longer deserve to be called your son; treat me as you would one of your hired workers.' "*Luke 15:17–19*

While the exchange between the father and his younger son reveals just how much God is ready to forgive, the scene involving the older brother discloses how hard it is for people who have been obeying God to be compassionate towards men and women who have deliberately and seriously failed. What example can Jesus set which once and for all will expose the insecurity and stinginess of righteous people? What example can God set in Jesus of a love and acceptance which truly knows no bounds?

The Church is not in the business of causing people to feel guilty about themselves in order to make them realize how much they need a messiah. There is nothing artificial about humanity's daily need for the creative, healing grace of God. Neither is Christian conversion just a momentary surrender to a moving sermon about Jesus and his message. Conversion means recognizing ourselves as sinners, and this recognition, or change of heart, opens us to the power of God's creative presence in our lives.

Why are we so slow to grasp the truth about ourselves? Perhaps because we fail to see that our sins really belong to us: the deed is ours, and what we do is a function of the person that we are. Our being, our true self, is not yet one with God because we have not allowed closeness to God to become a life-and-death matter for us. We do not yet speak to God, or trust God, or love God, out of that freedom and spontaneity, that intimacy and openness which characterized Jesus.

All of which is to say that Jesus was sinless and we are not.

The difference between us and Jesus is not something to be lamented or to feel guilty about, as if God has presented us with a model to which we shall never measure up. Nor should we permit Jesus' closeness to God to distance us from him. We must not stress Jesus' sinlessness or his oneness with the Father in ways which invite a steady comparison between him and us. Such thinking only produces discouragement. Whatever Jesus is, he is for our sake. Human beings are created in order to be bearers of the divine glory, and in Jesus God proves that this is possible. Human beings are created to be joined with God, and in Jesus God demonstrates that the human heart's deepest longing is not groundless. Jesus, God's Word made flesh, draws attention to the already and not-yet character of Christian existence. What Jesus already is, we hope to be, but we are not there yet.

4. *The death of Jesus*
Like every other human being, Jesus had to pass into that silent, unanswering and absolutely final moment of letting go. God did not reprieve him from the uncertainty, the torment, or the last minute anguish of feeling abandoned. His life's work at that point could hardly have seemed to be a success. His companions had fled, the once enthusiastic crowds had vanished, his adversaries had finally won the day. The skeptics among his followers had been proven right, and the kingdom of God had not arrived in any discernible form. He who had sounded and acted so sure, so confident of God's closeness, he who had spoken so charismatically and seemed unbeatable whenever he confronted religious hypocrisy or vested interests, this one is betrayed by a friend whom he had personally chosen. He is tried and condemned on trumped-up

charges; he is ridiculed, beaten, and publicly humiliated; he is officially rejected by the religious establishment, and then he is nailed to a cross. Matthew writes:

"Likewise the chief priests with the scribes and elders mocked him and said, 'He saved others; he cannot save himself. So he is the king of Israel! Let him come down from the cross now, and we will believe in him. He trusted in God; let him deliver him now if he wants him. For he said, I am the Son of God.' " *Matthew 27:41–44*

The end of Jesus' life scarcely seems to match its beginning. The end hardly appears to confirm the fact that God was well-pleased with Jesus, that Jesus was indeed the messenger of God's kingdom, or that Jesus had reaped any lasting fruit from fields which once looked so ripe for harvest.

What the story of Jesus reveals is that lives can be of God and still end in real failure. Do we believe in this Jesus, who had no choice at the end except to surrender himself into God's hands? Perhaps this is simply a way of asking, as we prepare to renew our baptismal promises: Are we willing to be drawn into Jesus' experience simply because his way is our only way to God? Are we ready to learn the lessons which his death teaches us about being human, and about living and dying into God?

Jesus died. By the time Jesus broke bread and gave the cup to his disciples at their final meal, he had realized that his life was coming to a close. "This is my blood of the covenant, which will be shed for many" (Mark 14:24). Luke makes this even more direct: "This cup is the new covenant in my blood, which will be shed *for you*" (Luke 22:20). And Matthew records why Jesus' life was being emptied: "for this is my blood of the covenant, which will be shed on behalf of many *for the forgiveness of sins*" (Matthew 26:28). The bread and cup here symbolize the whole of Jesus' life—not merely his physical self—but everything he did, and taught, and testified to. His life, all he experienced, his relationship with God, his compassion for all men and women, but especially for the poor, the socially and religiously marginalized, and those marked as sinners; his love and faith, his vision of the kingdom, his enthusiasm for the things of God, his very spirit: this is what the bread and cup now represent. His entire self, in other words, has already been given both for the disciples and for people of all time. The final pouring out sacramental-izes, as it were, the whole of Jesus' life for others. And why did he consent to what lay ahead? Why did he go through with it? The answer, as Matthew tells us, is simple: so that sins might be forgiven.

Jesus died. The Church can view his death from many perspectives. By dying, Jesus atoned for our sins. By dying, Jesus expressed a solidarity with victims of all time. In dying, Jesus takes our place; though innocent, he endures what the rest of us deserve for our sins. These are some ways of interpreting the death of Jesus. There are, however, a number of concrete reasons which brought Jesus to his death. Judas betrayed him. The scribes and Pharisees hated him. The imperial gov-ernment, which Pilate represented, refused him justice. And the official charge against him was political. His enemies said he claimed to be a king. It is ironic that the charge written above his head echoed the tempta-tion in the desert, the temptation to seize kingship: "All these I shall give to you!" Not for all the kingdoms in the world would Jesus choose a path other than the one along which God was sending him.

But that does not yet help us to see the connection between Jesus' death and the forgiveness of sins. We can picture soldiers preparing for battle, telling them-selves that if they should lose their lives, they will be doing so for the sake of their fellow citizens. Did Jesus view himself along such lines? Was he about to do battle with the power of darkness, and had he reached the conclusion that the only way to defeat that power was to surrender to it, trusting in the Father to do him justice? Did he thus think of his life now as a sacrifice to be poured out for many? Or perhaps Jesus anticipated his death as a prophetic gesture, like someone risking prison through civil disobedience, or like a person who stands in the way of an armed crowd in order to draw attention to the madness of violence. Was he haunted by the passages in Isaiah about God's suffering servant, the righteous one who suffers on behalf of his people?

One thing has to be certain. God did not demand the death of Jesus in order to begin forgiving us, or to open the gates of heaven, or to ransom us back from Satan. If God had not poured the Spirit into Jesus, if the Spirit had not made Jesus zealous for the things of God, then Jesus would never have led the kind of life he did. If God had not loved Jesus so much, then Jesus might have approached his mission with far less urgency. One thing we can say, therefore, is that Jesus died because he was a prophet. He testified to his knowledge and experience of God, and this experience undeniably brought him into conflict with anything which was not of God. People opposed him, he remained faithful to the Father, and he paid the price.

Compassion and selflessness marked Jesus' entire existence. The final pouring out of his life on the cross would make no sense apart from the history which preceded it and gave the cross substance. The cross would have no meaning if we did not know what Jesus was like during the years when he was fulfilling his mission. Jesus would have viewed his death as his last prophetic act, and as such it was also his last prayer. Although the disciples did not at first grasp this reality, they would keep recalling the death of Jesus and they would remember it precisely as an act of love. He loved them, and that is why he remained faithful to his mission, even when the opposition had hardened against him, even when his disciples abandoned him in their confusion and fright.

Forgiveness means knowing oneself as loved and accepted by God. Eventually the disciples did grasp this, precisely because Jesus was the sign of God's merciful closeness. They grasped that everything Jesus did, everything he was, was for them and for "the many." And why? Because they mattered to God; because Jesus truly loved them; because in his presence they felt themselves special; because in his company they felt themselves living openly and trustingly before God; because he would lay down his life in order to demonstrate what fidelity to God means. In this sense, Jesus' death was a sacrifice—a prayer, a trusting surrender—on our behalf. His death would say: If this is the only way for men and women to understand the destructiveness of sin, to see God's Son hanging shamefully from a cross, then so be it. If the cross alone can be the permanent sign in human history of God's unfailing love for the world, then let it be. His life poured out becomes the new covenant. His cross will forever express the unfathomable mystery of God's love for the world. To believe in Jesus is to understand that only God can break sin's power over human minds and hearts, and this is what God does through the crucified Jesus.

WHO ROSE FROM THE DEAD

The Church asks us further whether we believe in Jesus Christ who rose from the dead and is now seated at the right hand of the Father. This part of the formula contains two kinds of language: a faith statement (who rose from the dead) and a mythological statement (seated at the right hand of the Father). "Mythological" refers to the fact that the statement makes use of imagery to express this aspect of Christian belief; it does not imply fabrication or untruth. God, we realize, has neither a right hand nor a left, and Jesus is not literally sitting for all eternity on one side of God. "At God's right hand" symbolizes the honor and power the exalted Jesus now enjoys, echoing the words of the psalm, "The Lord said to my Lord: 'Sit at my right hand till I make your enemies your footstool' " (Psalm 110:1). The faith statement is telling us that Jesus did not raise himself (e.g., Acts 2:32). Or as Paul wrote, "Christ has been raised from the dead, the firstfruits of those who have fallen asleep" (1 Corinthians 15:20). The point is important, because it underscores the fact that Jesus was really dead. He could not have raised himself, any more than he could have missioned himself at the beginning of his public ministry. Like us, Jesus had to trust in the power and faithfulness of God. We have inherited and we believe the testimony of the apostles, those who witnessed the risen Jesus, when they insist that the same Jesus they walked with during his earthly life is now one with the Father. It may be tempting to imagine or speculate about what this union is like, yet we can do no more than say that Jesus is now one with the Father in a mystery of the deepest love.

It is not my intention to analyze the resurrection stories, or to review how scripture scholars and theologians have defended the truthfulness of the apostolic witness that Jesus has indeed been raised. In one way or another, belief in the resurrection is presupposed by everything we have said so far, and it will figure prominently in the next chapter. As we remarked earlier, the evangelists (the individuals or communities who wrote the gospels) composed their narratives from the perspective of Easter faith. And their faith in the risen Jesus, like ours, was most likely based on two things:

the testimony of the apostles and the first disciples who experienced Jesus after his death, and their own religious experience. They knew within themselves that a new life had begun. Their faith in the risen Jesus was confirmed by the freedom, the power, the joy, and the strength which they discovered because they were living, no longer for themselves, but for him: "He indeed died for all, so that those who live might no longer live for themselves but for him who for their sake died and was raised" (2 Corinthians 5:15).

What we are being asked is whether we believe that God raised Jesus from the dead. Do we accept the testimony of those first followers when they tell us they know for certain that the Father of Jesus Christ is not a God of the dead, but of the living? It is the resurrection that authenticates the life and teaching of Jesus. Without this, the course Jesus took is emptied of any revolutionary meaning. Otherwise, the cross, as Paul recognized, would be worthless and we would become the most foolish of people. "If Christ has not been raised, your faith is vain; you are still in your sins. Then those who have fallen asleep in Christ have perished. If for this life only we have hoped in Christ, we are the most pitiable people of all" (1 Corinthians 15:17–19). Everything Jesus stands for and all that his cross represents hinge on the Easter message.

And yet our faith in Jesus' resurrection is not like trusting the work of historians or archaeologists who tell us about the past. With the passing of time, we do not become historically distant from the resurrection the way we do with respect to everything else. Through the power of the Spirit and the preaching of the Church, the gospel never becomes an ancient artifact. There is a lifegiving dimension to the resurrection which endures from generation to generation, and which has been repeatedly confirmed in the experience of Jesus' followers. The resurrection of Jesus is not an

98

event that takes place alongside all others which make up human history. It does not fit into an historical catalogue of great human happenings. The resurrection can only be interpreted in terms of a profound desire, buried surely and deeply in the human soul, that death should not have the final word over us. That desire turns into hope, and hope matures into belief and conviction: we are being created for more than what we see. Against the background of this hope, the resurrection story appears more and more "natural," and the apostolic witness rings victoriously true. In a universe where God is revealed as the one who creates, what else would we expect?

NOTES

1. For example, see James D. G. Dunn, *Unity and Diversity in the New Testament* (Philadelphia: Westminster Press, 1977); Raymond Brown, *The Churches the Apostles Left Behind* (Mahwah, N.J.: Paulist Press, 1984); and Jerome Neyrey, *Christ is Community* (Wilmington: Michael Glazier, 1985).

2. Let me recommend several works here: Eamonn Bredin, *Rediscovering Jesus* (Mystic, Conn.: Twenty-Third Publications, 1986); Albert Nolan, *Jesus Before Christianity* (Maryknoll, N.Y.: Orbis Books, 1978); and a more technical study, Jon Sobrino, *Christology at the Crossroads*, trans. John Drury (Maryknoll, N.Y.: Orbis Books, 1978).

3. We find this special language in the Church's creeds. For example, the Chalcedonian creed of the fifth century confesses "our Lord Jesus Christ, the same perfect in divinity and perfect in humanity . . . one in being with the Father as to the divinity and one in being with us as to the humanity . . . in two natures, without confusion or change, without division or separation . . . He is not split or divided into two persons, but He is one and the same only-begotten, God the Word, the Lord Jesus Christ . . ." [*The Christian Faith,* ed. J. Neuner and J. Dupuis (Westminster, Md.: Christian Classics, 1972), pp. 147–48]. In a recent study, Daniel Helminiak interprets some of this special language in contemporary terms. Jesus Christ, the only-begotten Son of God, expresses historically what he is eternally, namely, his absolute oneness with the Father. "The Eternal Word's historical expression of himself would be absolute fidelity to the Father. And he would be absolutely faithful to the Father by being faithful to himself [as the Son]." See *The Same Jesus* (Chicago: Loyola University Press, 1986), p. 165.

Chapter Four

Do You Believe in the Holy Spirit?

Peter [said] to them, "Repent and be baptized every one of you, in the name of Jesus Christ for the forgiveness of your sins; and you will receive the gift of the Holy Spirit. For the promise is made to you and to your children and to all those far off, whomever the Lord your God will call." Acts 2:38–39

Inasmuch as the Son is God and from God, by nature, since he has been truly generated from God the Father, the Spirit is his own, and is in him and from him. Cyril of Alexandria[1]

Christian faith is trinitarian. We believe in a God who has been revealed to us as Father, Son, and Spirit. This is not an idea arrived at through philosophical speculation but through the Church's reflection on the mystery of God which we know in and through Jesus Christ. For us, God is not a faceless supreme being, nor an impersonal creative force. God for us is always the Father of our Lord Jesus Christ. The God of whom Jesus spoke and with whom he was in constant communion was the one he called *Abba*, as we have already seen. But the only way to know and experience God as Jesus did was, as the disciples learned, by being-with-Jesus. Jesus did not merely provide the disciples with fresh information about God. Rather, being-with-him made possible a totally new experience of God, a God who is revealed as having a Son.

Just as our belief in God as Father has a christological basis, so too does our belief in God as Spirit. We would not know who the Spirit is apart from Jesus. Summarizing Paul's theology, one contemporary New Testament scholar put the matter this way:

"In his life on earth Jesus was a man determined by the Spirit—he lived 'according to the Spirit' (Romans 1:3f.); but in the resurrection this relationship was reversed and Jesus became the determiner of the Spirit. In a sense we may say that Jesus was so wholly determined by the Spirit of God that the character of Jesus became the clearest possible visible expression of the Spirit— not merely his actions and words, but *Jesus himself* became *the* charisma of God. . . . [I]n Paul's view the man Jesus became a sort of funnel or nozzle through which the whole course of salvation history flowed— whatever flowed through that nozzle came out at the other end in the shape of Jesus, transformed into his image. . . . In Paul then *the distinctive mark of the Spirit becomes his Christness.* . . . The touch of the Spirit becomes finally and definitively the touch of Christ. . . . [A]s *the Spirit was the 'divinity' of Jesus, so Jesus became the personality of the Spirit.*"[2]

We know what Spirit means on the basis of what it does; and what the Spirit does is to form Christ in us, to confer upon our lives a Christ-character. The Spirit also confers a Christ-character on human history, principally through building up the body of Christ, which is the Church, and empowering it to live the gospel before the world. It is called the *Holy* Spirit. "Holy" initially would have meant "whole," "complete," "in no way defective,"and thus "perfect." The term naturally came to be applied to divinity, because what is divine could not lack any perfection; God had to be "holy." The term might also have been associated with healing. Thus, the Spirit makes human beings "holy," that is, whole and complete; it restores and heals them. Human beings are not whole or perfect, however, until they are fully fashioned into the image and likeness of God, as revealed to us through the life, death, and resurrection of Jesus. In the same way, human history will not be complete until Christ "is all and in all" (Colossians 3:11).

The Spirit is neither an impersonal power or faceless presence, nor simply a roundabout way of referring to God's outreach toward the world. As another contemporary theologian has written, "[T]he Spirit is divine love in person." The Holy Spirit is always "the Spirit of Jesus Christ, the Spirit who is inseparably connected with the person and work of Jesus and whose task it is to make the person and work of Jesus present in the church and the individual Christian and thus bring them to their completion."[3] Thus the face of the Spirit has to be Jesus, the one through whom divine love has been revealed and in whose likeness we are being created.

The Church asks us whether we believe in the Holy Spirit. We are not being questioned exactly as to whether we believe that there is a Holy Spirit. We are being asked whether we believe *in* the Holy Spirit. All believing, of course, is "in the Spirit," since it is the Spirit who empowers us to believe in the first place. Unless the Spirit prompted us, we would not be believers at all. The Spirit enables us to express our act of faith in the mystery of God.

Believing in the Spirit, however, usually means something more. It means that we take with utter seriousness the faith-realities of the Church, the communion of saints, the forgiveness of sins, the resurrection of the body, and everlasting life. For the Spirit is the personal energizing presence behind these realities. The Spirit makes church possible. The Spirit unites all the people of God, of every time and place, and makes them holy. It is the Spirit who continues to create our minds and hearts into the image and likeness of God. Without the Spirit, we would never be able to believe that God loves us in spite of our sinfulness. The Spirit will raise our bodies to be with Jesus. From the Spirit springs eternal life, that is, the life for which we are daily being created: a life in which our every desire to love and be loved will be satisfied, fully and forever. These faith-realities are not just pious ideas and romantic hopes. They are beliefs which govern the way that we live.

The gospel reading for the Fifth Sunday of Lent in the A cycle is the story of the raising of Lazarus (John 11:1–45). The reading for the B cycle is John 12:20–33, a passage in which Jesus predicts his death and states for us the essence of Christian wisdom:

"Amen, amen, I say to you, unless a grain of wheat falls to the ground and dies, it remains just a grain of wheat; but if it dies, it produces much fruit. Whoever loves his life loses it, and whoever hates his life in this world will preserve it for eternal life." *John 12:24–25*

Then Jesus adds: "Whoever serves me must follow me, and where I am, there also will my servant be" (John 12:26). Clearly, the theme of both of these readings is life: Jesus as the source of true life, and the paradox of discovering life in the process of letting-go of self, the mystery which Paul described as power being made perfect through weakness (2 Corinthians 12:9). As the church in its Lenten remembrance approaches Jesus' final days, it seems to be anticipating through these texts his victory over death. Not just over his own death, but over the power of death itself: over the power of everything in human life which would defeat us by spoiling our dreams and by compromising our resolution to change our ways. Jesus defeats death's power to cancel human efforts at loving and forgiving.

And death is powerful. It is death that whispers to us, "Why struggle, what difference will it all make?" Death asserts itself whenever a human being dares to be free, or to take a risk for the sake of the kingdom of God, by raising hundreds of objections and reminding us of past failures. It is death that whispers when we are striving to remain faithful to our belief, "Do you really think you matter all that much to God?" Death will not wait until the last hour of our lives to claim us. It wants to claim us now, and we yield to its power each time we grow more timid about living what we promised at baptism. Death tempts us not to take so seriously the challenge which Jesus sets with his poverty, his freedom, his zeal for the kingdom, and his prophetic boldness. Finally, death wins whenever men and women no longer dare to imagine what shape the kingdom of God might take among them, if only they had faith.

When Jesus said, "I am the resurrection and the life; whoever believes in me, even if he dies, will live, and everyone who lives and believes in me will never die" (John 11:25–26), he was not only referring to the possession of life beyond the grave. The words of Jesus can also refer to a life we experience here and now. The Spirit of Jesus in us keeps saying "No" each time death tempts us to surrender our hopes, our promises, our capacity to believe and to follow Jesus, or our power to recommit ourselves to living authentically. The soul's deepest desires and possibilities can always be revived, or "raised from the dead." Like Lazarus, we can be summoned back to life in this world.

The Spirit of Jesus, then, is the Lord and giver of life, not just of physical life but of eternal life. And eternal life—a qualitatively new way of being human and of relating to God—has already begun for those who believe in Jesus (John 3:36). Where do we learn about this new life and begin to experience it? The answer is the Church, that is, the community of Jesus' disciples. They are the ones who teach us about the Lord; they are the ones who testify, on the basis of their own experience, that Jesus is truly of God. The community of Jesus' disciples, alive through his Spirit, is the place where human beings discover that Jesus is the Messiah, the Son of God, and through this belief experience life in his name (John 20:31).

DO YOU BELIEVE IN THE HOLY CATHOLIC CHURCH? This can be an extremely painful question. "I want to believe in it," a person might answer. "I want to believe in everything the Church stands for; but I cannot accept its claim to be holy. I have not found it to be a place of freedom and charity. Most of my fights are not with pagans and atheists, but with people in the Church who claim to be Christian. We are not fighting to convert the world; we generally seem to be fighting among ourselves. How can I believe in the Church?"

But there are other aspects of the Church too. To some people the Church may be a refuge in a sea of confusion. It may be flawed, but it is humanity's last best hope because, even though the Church does not always live up to its ideals, at least those ideals still speak to the human heart and the Church has the courage to proclaim them. The Church is, after all, only a sign (and sometimes a weak one) of intimate union with God and of the unity of the whole human race.

Or the Church may be for some a genuine experience of human community, of men and women sharing faith and life, caring and forgiving, and reaching out to a suffering world. In their parishes they may have enjoyed sound preaching, prayerful liturgies, and been invited to participate in making decisions. Such people do not picture the Church so much as institution and structure, as hierarchy and cult, but as men and women whom God has called to follow Jesus.

The Church remains a mystery. It is holy, not because all its members are holy, but because God loves it, or perhaps we should say, because God loves us. God's love for us individually is not conditioned by how often or how rarely we sin, and God's love for the Church surely must be the same. For this reason, therefore, just as we have to learn how to accept one another, so too we have to be able to accept the Church. The Church is often rigid and slow to learn lessons from its own history. The Church at times seems to stifle creativity and imagination, and often appears to be on the defensive. It reacts to many issues out of fear and dread, as if always lamenting the world, human culture, and the human condition, and it seldom admits to having made a mistake. Still, it is this Church which continues to reflect the light of Christ before the world. The Second Vatican Council said:

"[T]he church, embracing sinners in her bosom, is at the same time holy and always in need of being purified, and incessantly pursues the path of penance and renewal. . . . By the power of the risen Lord, she is given strength to overcome patiently and lovingly the afflictions and hardships which assail her from within and without, and to show forth in the world the mystery of the Lord in a faithful though shadowed way . . ." *The Dogmatic Constitution on the Church*, #8

This is a humble, forthright statement. Yes, the Church includes sinners; it stands ever in need of repentance and renewal. Yes, unfortunately, the Church sometimes overshadows the mystery of Christ. Yet the Church moves through history as a pilgrim people, asking the world not to be distracted by its failures but to look at the purpose of its journeying. The Church tries to point people in the direction of God.

Church, of course, is more than buildings and parishes. People are accustomed to speaking of "the"

Church, having in mind more or less the official institution. But what makes this visible institution "Church" and thereby distinguishes it from other organizations is the Spirit of Jesus. It is the Spirit who calls us together, who sustains our common life, and who keeps us focussed on the Lord. The institutional Church is hierarchically structured and exhibits a variety of organizational elements. But church looked at as a community of disciples highlights the Church's personal and humanly inviting aspect. From this perspective the Church is an event as much as it is an institution. Church happens when men and women join together in the Spirit of Jesus. To cite a text from Paul: "The grace of the Lord Jesus Christ and the love of God and the fellowship of the Holy Spirit be with all of you" (2 Corinthians 13:13). Grace, love, and fellowship or communion: these are the essential moments of the event called church. Naturally there are many external features of the Church: its manner of worship, its moral teaching, its ministry, its doctrine, and so forth. These provide the Church with its historical identity and often with its aesthetic form. But the genuine beauty of the Church lies in the fact that it both discloses and communicates God's own life. The love which is God and which comes from God, the grace which is Jesus and which comes from Jesus, and the solidarity or communion which is the Spirit and which comes from the Spirit—these are what constitute the Church's mystery. Whatever beauty attaches to the Church's external features derives from this.

To say that we believe in the Church, therefore, is to affirm our belief in the power of the Spirit to create a truly God-centered community. To believe in the Church is to believe that God intends men and women to live in peace, justice, and love. Jesus told his followers that the only demonstration which would impress upon the world that he had in fact come from God was their unity and love for one another: "This is how all will know that you are my disciples, if you have love for one another" (John 13:35). And again: "that they may be brought to perfection as one, that the world may know that you sent me, and that you loved them even as you loved me (John 17:23). "That the world may know": the community of believers has been charged with proving by the way they live that Jesus is truly God's Son.

At the same time, our belief in the Church imposes a responsibility. We are the only ones who can prove to the world that Jesus did in fact come from God, that Jesus is who the Church claims him to be. The world's only route to unity and peace is through love and justice; there is no other way, except the artificial oneness based on treaties, military might, and mutual economic interests. A world longing for unity needs a sign that unity is indeed possible, for human beings do in fact belong to a single family and therefore should not live as strangers to one another. But it needs a lived demonstration that people can live in this world without exploiting one another, or threatening one another, or trapping one another with empty promises.

Concern for building Christian community and concern for the wider world are interrelated. The first leads into the second. How can we be disciples of Jesus and not be involved with the world around us? At the same time, our experience of the world's need for healing and grace ought to make us redouble our efforts at making the Church an unmistakable sign of the possibilities for genuine communion with others. If we believe in the Church, then we share the responsibility of building the Church and of being a "sign of contradiction" to the world. This we do in small steps. We start with our families, for that is where our sense of belonging to others begins and develops, and that is where Christian life must finally be expressed if men and women are going to be persuaded about the truthfulness of the gospel. Then in our neighborhoods, among those with whom we work, in our day-to-day dealings with people, we have to demonstrate convincingly that we are Christians. Do we live our faith? Do we act as believers? Do we speak with one another about our deep concerns and hopes, do we pray together? Do we sincerely pray for one another? Are we concerned enough about the quality of human life that we commit ourselves to work for justice? Do we honor our promises and do we tell the truth? Do we treat others fairly, do we dignify our labor by working honestly? Do the issues of disarmament and economic justice really matter to us? Are we capable of forgiving, or of patiently listening, or of standing by our religious and moral principles? Do we sense the evil of those things which prevent men and women from being fully human and truly free? If we believe in the Church, then we are committing ourselves to making the Church a compelling sign of God's presence in the world.

THE COMMUNION OF SAINTS

"Do you believe in the communion of saints?" The question sounds harmless enough. But like the other questions which the Church asks during the profession of faith, this one also bears upon the way we live as followers of Jesus. It leads us to reflect upon the Church's conviction that we are linked to men and women of faith who have gone before us. Yet this conviction can be dismissed rather quickly because it seems to relate very little to the daily business of Christian living.

The Second Vatican Council teaches that through the lives of the saints, the presence and face of God are vividly manifested. The union with God which we seek they now enjoy to the full, and from their place in glory they intercede on our behalf. We should cherish them as our friends, because they are friends of the same

Jesus whom we love. Particularly in the eucharistic liturgy, as we recall Mary, the apostles, and all the saints, the worshiping community becomes one with the saints in praising and thanking God through the Spirit. (Indeed, should we not confidently hope that members of our families and our close friends who have truly lived and died in the Lord also belong to the company of God's holy ones?) The life that we share as we take the eucharistic bread and cup is nothing less than the life of the risen Christ, which is of course the life of God. The Holy Spirit is the bond of life and love joining us with all the saints. In honoring their memory and celebrating their holiness, perhaps we will find the courage to believe that someday we too shall be part of their company.

Authentic veneration of the saints consists in "the intensity of our active love"; we honor them best when we imitate them in their loving, rather than by multiplying our devotional practices. The Council states: "For as long as all of us, who are sons [and daughters] of God and comprise one family in Christ remain in communion with one another in mutual charity and in one praise of the most Holy Trinity, we are responding to the deepest vocation of the Church and partaking in a foretaste of the liturgy of consummate glory" [The Dogmatic Constitution on the Church, #51]. And what is that vocation? The Church's deepest vocation is to be "a kind of sacrament or sign of intimate union with God, and of the unity of all mankind" [ibid., #1].

Perhaps we can say that the communion of saints is God's answer to Jesus' prayer for his disciples: "Father, they are your gift to me. I wish that where I am they also may be with me, that they may see my glory" (John 17:24). He is asking the Father to ensure that his followers pass from death to new life and share fully in his own intimate knowledge and love of God.

But Jesus is not only looking towards a future communion that must wait until the next life to be enjoyed. This is a prayer he makes for his sisters and brothers in every time and place. For he also asks, "so that they may all be one, as you, Father, are in me and I in you, that they may also be in us, that the world may believe that you sent me" (John 17:21). Given the background of the fourth gospel, we can say that here it is actually the glorified Jesus who is praying on our behalf.[4] He is asking the Father to keep his disciples faithful to him as they journey through this life. After all, what else is a disciple if not someone who is regularly found in the company of Jesus? The risen Jesus remains among us in the power of the Spirit; whenever we glimpse his presence or experience his power in our lives or in the lives of others, we are witnessing his glory. In short, in his prayer at the Last Supper Jesus is asking the Father to keep us faithful to our practice of discipleship, to strengthen us in our being-with-him. He is praying that the Father should confirm us in our faith by letting us see his glory, his oneness with the Father, even in the moment of his suffering and death.

The Church's belief in the communion of saints reminds us of the salutary fact that history neither begins nor ends with us. Our age is probably less receptive to the intuition behind the communion of saints than our ancestors. Although many people today have a healthy sense of solidarity with other men and women throughout the world, at the same time have we not to some extent also detached ourselves from our history and our tradition? Do we think and act as if we were the first and the last generation of Christians? If so, then the Church's awareness of the communion of saints— our solidarity in life and holiness, our connectedness with those human beings who walked through this world before us and remained faithful to the Lord— should not be allowed to slip from our memory. Not only would this lead to forgetting how the faith has been handed down to us. It would also mean losing the encouragement which comes from knowing that those who were once behind us are now ahead of us, urging us to remain faithful to what we have promised and assuring that nothing need separate us from the love of God.

THE FORGIVENESS OF SINS

"Do you believe in the forgiveness of sins?" This question also follows our profession of belief in the Holy Spirit and it thus implies that to believe in the Holy Spirit is to believe in the forgiveness of sins. After all, the risen Jesus appeared to his disciples, breathed on them and said, "Receive the Holy Spirit. Whose sins you forgive are forgiven them, and whose sins you retain are retained" (John 20:22–23). Jesus himself connected forgiveness with the gift of the Spirit.

But the purpose of the question is not just to remind us that Jesus has charged his community with the ministry of reconciliation. No one doubts that God will forgive us, and no one doubts that the Church is supposed to carry on Jesus' example of forgiving sins. (The experience of God's forgiveness, and the relationship between Jesus' death and the forgiveness of sins, need not be treated here; we touched on these in the last chapter.) Rather, to believe in the forgiveness of sins in the context of this question is to reaffirm the possibility of conversion and change of heart, as long as we are alive. It is to declare that the Spirit is continually working to create us and make us whole. Which means that the way we are is not the way we always have to be, because human beings are free. This freedom is itself a mystery, since here the creative power of God penetrates us silently, deeply, and often before we are ever aware of it. In short, the Church's belief that sins can be forgiven is a profound expression of Christian hope. It is a resounding affirmation of human possibility, or perhaps of divine possibility. As the angel assured Mary, "Nothing will be impossible for God" (Luke 1:37).

Sins can be forgiven: However far we stray, however dark the path along which we have wandered, however confused our faith or however unsteady our discipleship, however embarrassed and humiliated we are by what we have done, none of this is irreversible. Christians believe in the forgiveness of sins, that is, they are convinced that God never gives up creating us and redeeming our freedom. Thus the follower of Jesus should never yield to despair about personal failures. Each of us has his or her own particular faults and weaknesses; each of has our own pattern of sinfulness. For one it means battling against impatience or an unruly temper. For another it may be laziness or greed. For others it can be pride, or envy, or meanness, or the failure to be faithful to one's commitments. No matter how sin manifests itself in our lives, God still finds us. "For you darkness itself is not dark, and night shines as the day," wrote the psalmist (Psalm 139:12). Eventually we feel our sinfulness, that is, we feel life being sucked out of us, or we feel aimless, imprisoned, or just bored with living. Or our minds and hearts simply become dulled to the life of the Spirit. The vision of faith fades; realities which once felt so firm and clear no longer hang together. And yet, no situation in which we might conceivably find ourselves can be too sordid or unholy for God to be reaching out to us. God does not cease loving us because we do evil things. God can enter our lives through the frustration, the noise, and the hollowness which is human sin. How? By rekindling our heart's desire for freedom, for life, and for communion with others. Or by sending us men and women with whom we can unburden ourselves, or whose love and friendship encourage us to believe that change is always possible.

Our belief in the possibility of forgiveness reflects our confidence that if "God so loved the world that he gave his only Son" (John 3:16), then we are worth a great deal to God. In fact, we are worth a great deal even before we have taken the first step on the road to repentance and finding God. The Spirit enables us to be confident of this. Christians then have every reason not to yield to discouragement when their progress seems slight at best, or when they fail. Sin can be forgiven. I do not mean that we should live like people with an unlimited number of second chances. I mean that our belief about the forgiveness of sins is really not so much about us as about the patient love of God. God does not weary of us; we cannot tire God by our waywardness. But this truth about God must not be converted into an innocuous truism about divine mercy, either. While we may not be able to weary God, anyone who has taken a long, sober look at herself or himself has surely wondered whether life will amount to a hill of beans. We may well grow tired of ourselves. There is no cheap assurance that we shall never have to pay the price for our blindness and infidelity. Nevertheless, the Church still insists that God will always be there to forgive, provided of course that at some level we are honestly seeking to be free and to be whole.

Believing in the Holy Spirit commits us to reverencing human life, no matter how irreligious a person's life appears. For what we are believing in is the power of grace to touch and transform people, even when they have fallen into the darkest and most desperate conditions of which the human spirit is capable. It is easy to fall into the habit of thinking that grace reaches basically good people to make them better, which obviously it does. For the most part, the Church's ministry of reconciliation unfolds among those who have already been converted. Most of us would hardly qualify for one of the categories of notorious sinners. Yet if the gospels remember Jesus for anything, surely it is for his outreach to those who had wandered far from God. Besides, for Jesus no one belonged to the class of ordinary, everyday, run-of-the-mill sinners. In fact, those who regarded themselves as righteous appear to have had the least understanding of divine forgiveness and their consequent need for healing. For Jesus, all stand in need of divine mercy and compassion. It follows, then, that the Church can never write off those who are most distant from God, those who are most alienated from the self or person which God calls them to be. And neither can we. The community undertakes the ministry of reconciliation because of its profound regard for human life.

Not only do we associate the Spirit with forgiveness. The Spirit is also the driving force behind Christian mission. Although this is not expressly mentioned in the profession of faith, we should reflect on it briefly in connection with forgiveness. To believe in the Holy Spirit, and therefore in the forgiveness of sins, is also to accept the mission which outwardly expresses that belief. With St. Paul we can say that to us has been entrusted the ministry of reconciliation (2 Corinthians 5:19). This means that the Christian community (and each of us in the measure that we can do so) has the special charge of breaking down whatever barriers keep people alienated from one another and from God, for alienation in any form is the dehumanizing effect of sin. This, after all, is what Jesus did. Affirming as we do the Church's faith in the possibility of redemption for every human being, no matter how firmly sin has taken hold, requires us to help others escape the dehumanizing effects of sin. If the conditions in which people live are robbing them of their freedom and spontaneity, then the Christian community cannot stand by idly waiting for God to change things. If people cannot escape the cycles of poverty and violence which breed broken human lives, then the community of Jesus' disciples will feel themselves drawn by the Spirit to help them. Whatever form alienation takes—poverty, injustice, ignorance, a loss of the sense of God—the disciples of Jesus will be working to overcome it.

A basic condition of being a disciple of Jesus is the readiness to forgive one another. We are reminded of this each time we recite the Our Father, or when we listen to texts such as: "If your brother sins, rebuke him; and if he repents, forgive him. And if he wrongs you seven times in one day and returns to you seven times saying, 'I am sorry,' you should forgive him" (Luke 17:3–4). And again:

"Then Peter approaching Jesus asked him, 'Lord, if my brother sins against me, how often must I forgive him? As many as seven times?' Jesus answered, 'I say to you, not seven times but seventy-seven times' " *Matthew 18:21–22*

Readiness to forgive, however, is not all that is expected of us. The follower of Jesus does not sit passively until a brother or sister comes seeking forgiveness. There is the additional step of initiating the process of reconciliation, just as Jesus actively sought out and tried to save what was lost (Luke 19:10). Perhaps this means going out of our way, insofar as we can, to be peacemakers, or helping to repair broken relationships, or comforting those who have lost their self-respect, or reassuring one another of the reality of God. It may even mean confronting evil situations so that people become aware of their moral blindness or their spiritual helplessness. It makes little sense to declare our belief in the forgiveness of sins and then do nothing while people remain trapped in their sin, or their guilt, or their alienation, or their fear. The Spirit

prompts us beyond verbal declaration; our belief must
be put into practice. As the community of Jesus' disciples, his Spirit impels us to bring others to understand
how much they matter to God. Our concern becomes
their sign of God's own concern. As followers of Jesus,
we must help others to hope, as we hope for ourselves,
that so long as we draw breath we can respond to
God's creative power to make us fully human and fully
free.

THE RESURRECTION OF THE BODY

At the time of Jesus, many people in Israel believed in a
general resurrection of the dead at the end of the
world, and Jesus naturally shared that belief. One gospel text recalls his being questioned by some Sadducees, who denied the resurrection; they were attempting to trick him with a thorny problem about a woman
who had seven husbands. For Jesus, the Sadducees
understood neither Scripture nor the power of God,
and he silenced them by answering, "He is not the God
of the dead but of the living" (Matthew 22:32). Later
Paul would argue that if there is no resurrection of the
dead, then Christ has not been raised (1 Corinthians
15:13). For Paul, it is the possibility of the general resurrection at the end of time which renders intelligible
Jesus' being raised from the dead within the course of
human history. The resurrection of Jesus confirms the
fact that God indeed creates us for life. Jesus' resurrection is a sign that our hope in God's creative power to
bring us into everlasting life and communion has not
been misplaced.

Yet there is a difference between the bodily resurrection of Jesus and our own. His resurrection has already
been accomplished, but ours waits until the end of
time. While Paul conjectures in broad strokes about the
nature of our risen bodies (see 1 Corinthians 15:42–51),
he cannot say much more than that what is mortal will

117

be swallowed up by life (2 Corinthians 5:4–5), or that even now we are being transformed (or, as we might also say, being created): "All of us, gazing with unveiled face on the glory of the Lord, are being transformed into the same image from glory to glory, as from the Lord who is the Spirit" (2 Corinthians 3:18). Christ will change our mortal bodies so that they conform with his glorified body (Philippians 3:21).

The disciples of Jesus would likewise have shared the hope of a general resurrection of the righteous, although they do not appear to have anticipated witnessing the powerful reality of that hope so soon. They misunderstood Jesus' prediction about his own resurrection, a prediction which most likely grew out of his profound confidence that God would not allow his mission simply to end with humiliation and death. It was absolutely imperative that God raise Jesus within human history, and not merely at the end of time, in order to leave Jesus' followers with a compelling sign as to which side God had taken in humanity's battle against injustice.

Because we are human, we necessarily live in relation to others and to the world of matter around us. To believe in the resurrection of the body is to expect that someday we shall enter a new, largely unimaginable relationship with one another, enjoying a form of redeemed bodiliness, as men and women fully created. I hesitate to speculate; perhaps we can do little more than articulate the hope underneath this belief, and maybe look for some clues in the story of Jesus' transfiguration. In any event, the prospect of death—its finality, the sense of loneliness and isolation it evokes, our complete separation from life and people—would paralyze us if we stared at it too long. That is why we need to meditate on Jesus' words that God is a God of the living. Such was Jesus' experience of God, and it must be ours as well. The only route out of "the long loneliness" is genuine communion with others. Where communion is genuine, people do not seek each other merely to escape from their fears, their isolation, or their boredom. Instead, they are drawn to one another out of real love and feeling, out of their need for acceptance and a readiness to pour out their lives for each other. In this world, living for others liberates us so that we are not paralyzed by death's sting. People who are increasingly absorbed by the mystery of love will apprehend the Christian truth that our God is a God of the living, not of the dead, and they will know this experientially. For them, the resurrection of Jesus sacramentalizes for all time God's unfailing love. It announces that whatever love and communion we crave and experience here will one day find its fulfillment in the kingdom of God.[5]

RESURRECTION FAITH AS COUNTER-CULTURAL
"Do you believe in the resurrection of the body and life everlasting?" This may very well be the most counter-cultural of Christian beliefs. It contradicts everything which pressures us into behaving as if the present life is all there is. Religion has long been accused of turning people's attention away from this world, especially from its pain and misery, with promises of everlasting bliss in heaven. Needless to say, Christianity has from time to time overstressed the evils that beset life in this world. The suffering of the present, we are told, is nothing compared to the glory which will be ours. And that is correct. But it is one thing to encourage such hope among those who are enduring persecution for their faith, or who are suffering unjustly and are powerless to prevent it, and another thing altogether to soothe those already living comfortably with dreams of an even more comfortable afterlife. It is one thing to draw strength from our conviction that just as Jesus was raised from the dead, so too shall we be raised, provided, of course, we remain faithful to him; and

another thing to be lulled with bright promises of immortality into a sleepy non-resistance to present evils.

Christian belief in eternal life should never render us oblivious to the challenges and responsibilities of being mature human beings in this world. If Jesus' sole concern had been the world to come, then instead of healing the sick he ought simply to have prepared them for a happy death. His outrage over injustice, his repeated warnings against the rich, in fact the vision behind Matthew 25 where Jesus identified himself with those who are hungry, imprisoned, naked, thirsty, and homeless, underscore for his disciples just how much they must do in this world, or else for them there will be no eternal life. Eternity almost sounds like an afterthought; Jesus is far more concerned about what happens on earth. His preaching, his teaching, his parables and miracles, have reference to the kingdom of God which is already unfolding in our midst. Even John's gospel, which speaks so much about eternal life, stresses that eternal life has already begun; the community of Jesus' disciples has already started to experience life in the Spirit.

Our belief in everlasting life should not sidetrack us from being seriously engaged with earthly concerns. The Second Vatican Council's Pastoral Constitution on the Church in the Modern World is a resounding affirmation of the Christian commitment to this task. The Council states:

"Pursuing the saving purpose which is proper to her, the Church not only communicates divine life to men [and women], but in some way casts the reflected light of that life over the entire earth. This she does most of all by her healing and elevating impact on the dignity of the person, by the way in which she strengthens the seams of human society and imbues the everyday activity of men with deeper meaning and importance. Thus, through her individual members and her whole community, the Church believes she can contribute toward making the family of man and its history more human." [#40]

And further in the same decree, speaking about the proper development of human culture, the Council continues:

"In every group or nation, there is an ever-increasing number of men and women who are conscious that they themselves are the artisans and the authors of the culture of their community. Throughout the world there is a similar growth in the combined sense of independence and responsibility. Such a development is of paramount importance for the spiritual and moral maturity of the human race. This truth grows clearer if we consider how the world is becoming unified and how we have the duty to build a better world based upon truth and justice. Thus we are witnesses of the birth of a new humanism, one in which man is defined first of all by his responsibility toward his brothers [and sisters] and toward history." [#55]

According to the Council, Christians have an obligation to collaborate with all men and women in constructing a more human world (ibid., #57). God intends us to be fully human and fully free, but the process of humanization cannot be achieved in circumstances which are essentially dehumanizing. If we are to be "artisans of a new humanity," therefore, we must throw ourselves into the work of improving, reforming, and rebuilding the political, social, and economic order. Since human beings not only create culture but are also created by culture, they have the responsibility of fashioning a culture which puts people in touch with their deepest aspirations and their true selves. Whatever alienates people from one another, or from their true self, cannot be of God. Values, structures, or practices which marginalize people, break down community, and rob people of their dignity and self-respect must be re-formed or overturned.

Christian faith holds most strongly to its belief in a life to come, and at the same time it works relentlessly to renew this world. The fact is that God created—and continues to create—a material universe. This means that Christians cannot sidestep their responsibility to help build a more human world by claiming that their business lies with the world to come. The reason for this is Easter faith, for the bottom line is that God raised Jesus from the dead; and that event provides the basis for Christian commitment and action. The risen Jesus remains present in this world through the Spirit, leading and strengthening his disciples as they con-tinue his work. The Spirit of the risen Jesus drives his followers into the world and human society, not away from it.

God did not raise Jesus from the dead in order to as-sure us that everything will be fine, that death is an illusion. Easter is not God's way of relieving us from worrying about what comes after this life, or of comfort-ing us as we mourn the death of our loved ones, or of spurring us to virtue with the prospect of reward. What informs our belief in the resurrection of the body and life everlasting is divine justice. That is the heart of the matter. God decrees that we act justly, and because of Jesus' resurrection we can expect that God will do justice toward us.

God raised Jesus from the dead because God is a God of justice. Justice—the very justice which God exacts of us through the prophetic voices of the Old Testament—demands that God not abandon Jesus to the grave, nor allow his body to undergo decay (Acts 2:31). Jesus was God's faithful servant. He lived and died solely for God, and the suffering which he encountered would never have happened had God not been at the center of his life. Having heard the story of Jesus, and especially having listened carefully to the account of his suffering and death, everything inside us clamors for justice. And God answers, not just us but Jesus himself who cried to God in his moment of abandonment, by raising him from the dead. In the case of Jesus, God could not remain silent; otherwise, the victory of injustice would have been intolerable, and the devil, who could not conquer Jesus in the wilderness, would have vanquished him in the end.

What commends our belief in the resurrection of the body, then, is our grasp of divine justice, which is intensified by our experience of widespread injustice throughout the world. So many go hungry; so many rot in prisons though they have committed no crimes; so many families destroyed by war; so many victims of avarice and political oppression; so many innocent people forced to pay the consequences of ideological conflict between the superpowers. In addition to this there are the broken bodies—innocent people born deformed, retarded, diseased, maimed,—and the broken spirits—people whose political, social, and economic backgrounds have torn away their will to live, imprisoned them in ignorance or cycles of violence and fear, or crushed their spontaneity and their dreams. Contemplating the human condition this way strains our faith and drives us to shout to God, perhaps echoing the exasperated faith we hear in some of the psalms. Looking at people who are broken and wounded, who of us has not stood before God puzzled, maybe even enraged, over the evil, the misfortune, and the injustice which produces so much suffering? Not only do we feel ourselves compelled to work among and for such people in whatever ways we can, not only do we know that our faith is meaningless if it fails to involve us in doing justice; but our hearts cry out for resurrection.

What horrible burdens some men and women are forced to bear![6]

Surely the same feelings must have stirred through the heart of Jesus when he saw the blind, the lame, the diseased, the destitute people of his day. Surely the same outrage must have burned in his soul when he saw the cruelty, the unfeeling cynicism of the rich and powerful against those who were poor and defenseless. When he taught about ultimate judgment and justice, he may have used images of banquets and celebration, but his purpose was hardly to soften people's suffering and make them forget their desperate condition. He was indicting the wealthy, established classes of his day, in their callous disregard for those who did not belong to their class, or in their simple failure to notice who their neighbors really were. In other words, Jesus' preaching about eternal life was based on a profound intuition about divine justice.

Easter faith is not a candied word to keep us from complaining. It was born out of the depths of human anguish and it affirms the profoundest of human hopes. Jesus' resurrection, which has to be the starting point for all of the Church's reflection about our resurrection and eternal life, inaugurated a brand new way of his being present to his disciples. This is not the place to enter into a discussion about what happened on Easter morning, or about the nature of Jesus' risen body. By way of summary I think it can safely be said that the New Testament writers were not all that concerned about these issues. They simply tell us what they did know and experience: that those who came to visit his tomb several days after burial discovered it was empty; that the resurrection was not all that easy for them to comprehend. Apparently, despite whatever Jesus may have predicted, they did not anticipate a resurrection. They "saw" him afterwards, but his physical appearance was clearly different; it took a word, or a familiar gesture, or some sign from Jesus before they could recognize him. They tell us that he had empowered and sent them to carry on his work; that he loved them more than they ever realized before his death.

Essentially, the disciples experienced Jesus still present in their midst, particularly in "the breaking of the bread," drawing them together, strengthening and inspiring them, opening their minds to the dimensions of God's kingdom, and reminding them of the things he had taught. This describes their experience of Jesus in this world. They have nothing to tell us about how our resurrection will take place, any more than they could tell us how Jesus' resurrection took place. They have little to add to Jesus' own images about everlasting life as an eternal banquet. Yet even Jesus' images should not be read too literally. He was probably no more describing what our final union with God will be like than his images of hell reveal what eternal loss is. I suspect he simply intended to make people serious about repenting and believing the gospel.

As noted above, the Church's belief in the resurrection of the body and eternal life is counter-cultural. It is counter-cultural in a broad sense because the passionate pursuit of justice often runs against the political and financial interests of many people. They do not feel strongly about the world's poverty, its political and economic instability, except insofar as such conditions could destabilize the structures which protect their security and well-being. For them, resurrection faith sounds like frosting on the cake; it surely is not grounded in a profound sense of solidarity with the underprivileged majority of the human race. When the Church preaches the resurrection of Jesus, therefore, it is implicitly teaching about divine justice. After all, it was the *crucified* Jesus who was raised. While I would not be so bold as to suggest that the poor have *merited* everlasting life (eternal life has to be God's gift), I do regard with utmost seriousness the words of Jesus that it is easier for a camel to pass through the eye of a needle than for the rich to enter the kingdom of God. Further, I believe that those who suffer unjustly have a claim on God which demands that God raise them up, and I take the death and resurrection of Jesus to be the evidence. Throughout salvation history, God has demonstrated where the divine loyalties lay. We have but to read Luke 1:46–55, the *Magnificat* of Mary, to see how deeply rooted in the Church's memory is the direction of God's loyalty.

But our belief in the resurrection of the body and life everlasting is counter-cultural in another sense too. If we truly believe that our bodies will be raised and that this life foreshadows what is to come, then what impact does this have upon the way we live? Christians, like everyone else, are people of their times. Like everyone else, they are affected by, and indeed to a large extent formed by, their culture. The values and attitudes of our society sweep us along. Not only is it difficult to resist the currents of our age, but we are not always capable of distinguishing the positive from the seductive forces which play on us. It is easy to take the familiar situation as the real and normal situation for human living.

It may sound trite, but we must continually be asking ourselves whether we have been co-opted by the consumerist, individualistic mentality of our society. We spend vast amounts of money and time pampering our bodies. We cultivate health because we idealize being youthful, and this of course directly contradicts our belief that this body must die if it is to be raised to new life. By the way we live we pretend that we shall survive forever with the bodies we now have. Many people do not have a clue as to what makes men and women truly strong, truly beautiful.

The difficulty is not that our culture tends to deny the reality of death. Rather, it is that our culture has absolutely no understanding of the hope which underlies our belief in the resurrection of the body. And many Christians have succumbed to this impoverishment of their faith. Do we worry about what we are going to wear? Do we keep looking for the perfect diet, the one that will keep us free from various diseases? Do we turn away from physically unattractive people because they lack alertness, stamina, and beauty, or because they are ill or deformed? I am not advocating that Christians cease caring for their health; I am simply wondering whether we care about our health for its own sake, or whether we view physical well being as instrumental to serving one another.

This portrait of the ills of our times may sound worn and repetitious. It simply rehearses the familiar list of complaints against modern society. Yet however familiar the criticisms sound, they are not any the less well founded. To believe in the resurrection of the body is to espouse a conviction which is plainly counter-cultural. To believe that God is making us for eternity is to adopt a perspective which many human beings today do not share, at least not in any meaningful way.

We cannot profess our faith in the Spirit who will raise our bodies to be with Christ without examining ourselves. Would someone looking at us conclude that the way we live only makes sense because of our faith in everlasting life? Do those who call themselves Christians today stand apart from everyone else because their values are founded upon the fact that God raised Jesus from the dead? Or do our attachments, our anxieties, our preoccupations, our standards for praise and blame, our manner of living, the clothes we wear and the food we eat, our recreation, the things we talk about, do all these things indicate that we prefer the security and reality of the present to the promise of God revealed in Christ? Are we in effect saying, "Let's take what we can now, and if there is more to come later, then that will be a bonus?" If we live as if there will be no resurrection, then we shall have settled our future. For those who live as if there is nothing more, then for them this life may indeed be all they will have. "My child, remember that you received what was good during your lifetime, while Lazarus received what was bad; but now he is comforted here, whereas you are tormented" (Luke 16:25). Lazarus is not credited with anything more than having suffered bad things, that is, with having been poor. In justice, then, God raises him. But the wealthy provide God nothing worth raising up. They die and their memories are slowly erased from the history of the human race. Fully to live with Easter faith demands a new birth, a new way of perceiving and evaluating everything. That is what it means to believe in the Holy Spirit.

NOTES

1. Henry Bettenson, ed., *The Later Christian Fathers* (Oxford: Oxford University Press, 1972), p. 266.

2. James D. G. Dunn, *Jesus and the Spirit* (Philadelphia: Westminster Press, 1975), p. 325. See also Kilian McDonnell, "A Trinitarian Theology of the Holy Spirit," *Theological Studies* 46:2 (1985), pp. 191–227, especially pp. 204ff.

3. Walter Kasper, *The God of Jesus Christ*, trans. Matthew J. O'Connell (New York: Crossroad Publishing Co., 1984), pp. 227, 209.

4. Raymond Brown writes: "The Jesus who speaks here [in the Last Discourse] transcends time and space; he is a Jesus who is already on his way to the Father . . . Although he speaks at the Last Supper, he is actually speaking from heaven; although those who hear him are his disciples, his words are directed to Christians of all times. . . . [F]or whatever there may be of the *ipsissima verba* in the Last Discourse has been transformed in the light of the resurrection . . ." *The Gospel According to John XIII–XXI* (Garden City, N.Y.: Doubleday & Co., 1970), pp. 581–582.

5. See Gerald O'Collins, *Jesus Risen* (Mahwah, N.J.: Paulist Press, 1987), pp. 188–200.

6. The connection between resurrection and justice has been important in liberation theology. See Jon Sobrino, *Christology at the Crossroads*, trans. John Drury (Maryknoll, N.Y.: Orbis Books, 1978): "The hermeneutic locale for understanding the resurrection of Jesus is not to be found simply in hope. It is to be found in the questioning search for justice in the history of suffering" (p. 244). See also Sobrino, *Jesus in Latin America* (Orbis Books, 1987), pp. 148–158.

Imaging Christian Mission

Whoever serves me must follow me, and where I am, there also will my servant be.   John 12:26

The promises we make at baptism and renew through-out our lives will determine the kind of people we be-come, provided we take those promises seriously. Christian belief needs to be reflected upon and contem-plated, if we are to profit from its power to nourish our minds and hearts. But Christian belief should also move us to act. In fact, there are some aspects of Chris-tian faith we shall never understand until we put them into practice. Talk about forgiveness remains merely that until we actually have to forgive someone. Talk about keeping commitments or trusting in God is only a matter of words until we are actually faced with hav-ing to stand by our promises or to depend entirely upon the Lord. Yet Christian practice is not a matter of proving to God or to ourselves that we are believers. On the contrary, it is by doing Christian things that we apprehend the truth of Christian belief. We are believ-ers because we have learned experientially that the Christian way is lifegiving. Or, to be as elementary as possible, there is no such thing as a purely theoretical knowledge of Jesus; the only way to know him is to follow him.

Having been baptized, what is our mission? What does the Lord expect us to do? For each person the answer will be somewhat different. In general terms, Jesus expects us to be the light of the world, the salt of the earth, or the city set on a hill. He expects that his disciples will be a visible, effective presence in the world, bearing witness to him by their faith, their hope, their action, and their love. Specifically, each of us has to discern what being faithful to the Lord means in the particular circumstances of his or her own life. Given the responsibilities we have toward our families or in our jobs, or given the physical constraints and psychological limitations under which we have to live, or given our individual talents and weaknesses, what concretely ought to be the path of our discipleship?

In trying to discern what following the Lord is going to mean for us, it might help to engage in an imaginative exercise. "Where I am, there also will my servant be." The point is not that Jesus should be where we are, but rather that we are to be where he is. Well, then, where is Jesus? Where do we imagine him to be? How might we conceive his presence among us today? In answering this we may begin to form a clearer picture of Christian mission.

Odd as it may seem, some people find it difficult to imagine Jesus as a truly historical person. He may be a person, but he also appears to be someone without a real place in space and time, and thus without a credible humanity. He appears to them more divine than human, more other-worldly than this-worldly, more a treasured possession of the Church than a reality flowing out of their own lives. What they know of his life is segmented through the different gospel texts they have listened to at church, and this makes their picture of him too still and artificial. As a result, Jesus feels more distant to them than, say, Mary, or even the Father. How does one follow that kind of Jesus with all the passion and energy of someone in love?

I think the solution to this problem lies in a prayerful, imaginative entry into the gospel story, although the only defense of this claim I can offer is a personal one. Some years ago, before modern scriptural studies began to make their impact, I stumbled across the two volumes of Archbishop Alban Goodier's *The Public Life of our Lord Jesus Christ*. Goodier had the ability to draw his readers into the gospel scenes so that the parables, the healings, the exchanges between Jesus and his disciples felt vividly alive. In those books one wandered imaginatively and freely through the life of Jesus. You walked down roads and felt the hot dusty wind against your face and arms. You stood silently as Jesus healed a paralytic, and gasped with the crowd when an epileptic regained his senses. The scene of the two disciples following Jesus along the riverbank, their asking "Where do you live?" and his answering "Come and see," seemed breathtakingly close. Goodier brought his reader to that spot by the Jordan and through the pages of the book Jesus, you could be certain, had caught sight of you. The homes, the faces of the people, the tone of the disciples' questions, the blue of the water in the Lake of Galilee, the hillside where he delivered the Sermon on the Mount, the road from Jerusalem to Jericho, the tears of the woman who wept at his feet, the grainfields through which he walked, his encounters with the rich young man, and the woman at the well, the smell of wineskins and harvests—the reader's imagination turned pilgrim, pausing everywhere and lingering over the details. You might find yourself stopping to re-read portions of those volumes so that there would always be more to come. Goodier invited your imagination into contemplating Jesus along the road, at the lakeside, in the upper room. You watched him pray and saw how he touched, how he embraced, how he forgave, and afterwards relished the memory of it all. From then on, you knew him, and although you might not yet fully know yourself, you knew that your life had been changed for good.

I appeal to this recollection of Goodier in order to defend my conviction that we need an imaginative entry into the gospels if Jesus is to be a person fully inserted into everyday life. We must think of him as a real flesh-and-blood person if he is truly going to win our hearts. One should not be distracted with questions about the historical reliability of various gospel texts, because such questions are beside the point here. To be sure, the old "lives of Christ," including Goodier's, which were once so popular, have been outdated by contemporary biblical scholarship. But the gospels themselves have, if anything, become even more exciting, richer, and more firmly rooted in the human story as a result of modern research. They invite us into the experience and imagination of Jesus. Although we may have been used to reading the gospels as accounts of Jesus' life, we have learned that in fact they are more accurately stories of Jesus in the lives of his disciples. Perhaps this is what makes Mark's story of Jesus so vigorous, so compelling. The Jesus who teaches and heals in Mark reaches us through the recognizable features of his all too human disciples. And this means that the only life of Christ which can be written is the life of Christ in us. The Jesus reached by our imaginations turns out to be amazingly near.

Our imaginations can, and should, penetrate the gospel texts to see and touch the person of Jesus, yet in the end we have to return to our own world, which is not the world of first-century Palestine. In our world, and surely in our culture, people do not ride donkeys or wash their guests' feet; there are few shepherds, or lepers, or kings, or Roman centurions. As we read the texts or as the Church preaches them, we have to transpose those foreign elements and let the gospels speak to us in our context. In other words, we interpret.

What would Jesus say to the rich young man today? What images would he employ to portray the kingdom of God? How might he tell the story of the good Samaritan? And so forth.

But in addition, the exercise of leaping across two thousand years into the gospel scenes would lock us into the past unless it were sustained by the fact that the Jesus who appears there was raised from the dead. That person is as much a part of our century as he was of the first. We learn of him through the Church, we contemplate him on the pages of the New Testament, our imaginations reach out to him and let us relive the events we read about. "I am with you until the end of the world" is not merely a past promise remembered but an experience of the risen Jesus which continues from one age to the next. This means that there are people today who experience Jesus as surely and really as the Christians of the first century. The passion with which they live their faith can bring other people to discover him too, or to renew their practice of discipleship. What happened twenty centuries ago still attracts, challenges, and transforms ordinary human beings like us.

Where do we image Jesus? Again, permit me to be personal. There is a hill overlooking the city where I live, an older industrial New England city. From there, sitting on some outcropping of rock, one can survey the city from the brow of the hill. Like a camera panning a broad and particularly detailed picture, one's attention can rotate leisurely and fondly over the scene below. And the city, which from the hillside feels so serenely in place, gradually defines itself. The mind leaves its outpost and begins to wander down the hill, across the expressway, around abandoned factories, along the main streets, and into the neighborhoods. You imagine your way inside the graying three-story apartments in order to watch and to listen. People are either cooking or eating, some are sleeping or making love, some are arguing and crying, others are sitting idly on front steps or just keeping an eye on children playing on the sidewalks. In one area a few young boys hustle drugs on the street, and poor women keep appointments with their male customers. People are strolling in and out of shops, some are working in office buildings, others roam the area aimlessly.

A large downtown mall houses a number of department stores. Besides the shoppers, there are the sightseers who have parked themselves on a bench indoors because they are inveterate people watchers, or maybe because they are old or unemployed and have nothing better to do, or because in the winter they want to escape the cold, and in the summer the heat, or maybe they just need to escape their loneliness. Your attention moves toward the hospitals where it is easy to imagine what is happening on the various floors. People are recovering from surgery, or being sustained on life-support systems, or have checked into the emergency rooms with sick, crying children, or are lying in bed and dreaming about being discharged. There are many churches in the city, but they feel quiet and empty, more reminders of the religiousness of a former age than places which still center the presence of God. Within moments, the whole scene starts to feel sacred. Perhaps that is because the mystery of the incarnation is saying something to the imagination. The scene feels sacred because God is down there, in those apartments, on those streets, hovering namelessly around people who may not have even the foggiest notion about who God is.

What would Jesus have done or said if he were passing through the city? Would he mount a box on a street corner and begin to preach? Would he stop and horse around with some of the children? Would he perform a miracle or two to attract attention? Would he go into one of the taverns, study the men and women standing around the bar, and then invite a few of them to join him in working for the kingdom of God? Would he find some of his future apostles in the mall, or among the teenagers playing basketball behind one of the high schools? Would he come crashing into the routine of a banker or lawyer on the way to lunch, or capture the attention of the road crew repairing potholes? Would he be speaking Spanish? Would one of the prostitutes stare at him, trying to size him up, and would he look with such compassion at her that she would break down in tears, or hide her face in shame?

Six days out of seven, where in the city would one expect to find him? In one of the banks, or at the city court, or waiting outside someone's office? Or would he be on a park bench surrounded by a crowd, or sipping coffee at a kitchen table in one of those gray apartments? Would he organize a Bible study group? Would he spend one day a week in some of the suburban towns, or meeting university professors? What sort of people would be likely to share his interest in the things of God? Would his manner be too refined for blue collar workers in one of the factories, or would he be too blunt and unschooled to be accepted by the professionals? Would his stories and parables sound too unsophisticated for university-educated people? How would he explain what he meant by the reign of God? Would he stop in a church to attend a service, and if he did, would he be satisfied by what he observed? Would his freedom offend the local clergy?

What kind of people would he be having dinner with tonight? He is reported many times to be at table with his friends, or with strangers, or with notorious sinners. Meal times were special to him. "A glutton and a drunkard," they used to call him, "a friend of tax collectors and sinners." "This man welcomes sinners and eats with them," the gospel reminds us. Would he dare enter a gay bar, and if he did, how would he open a conversation with the men he met there? Might the Lazarus he would have restored to life have died from AIDS? The gospels never mention that Jesus actually visited a prison, but given his words "I was in prison and you visited me," he surely must have done so. What might he have said to the inmates? Can we picture him in a taxi, or boarding a bus? Somehow it is hard to imagine him driving his own car. Would he recognize drug addicts as the modern form of people possessed by demons, and would he have demonstrated his power over evil by driving them out? What would Jesus do down there, in the city sprawled out before us? Where would he steal away to pray? Would he know that we were sitting at the top of a hill contemplating his movements, trying to listen in as he talked, guessing at where he would go next?

Would he lose his life in the city? And if so, who are the ones most likely to want his death, the ones most ready to take offense at his teaching, or his freedom, or his choice of friends? Who would have most to lose by taking up his challenge? Whose financial interests would be most threatened by his teaching? Drug pushers and pimps? People who work in the design and manufacture of weapons, or in the financial industry? Middle-class people climbing the social ladder? Fundamentalists who did not find him to be sufficiently ascetical or preaching enough about religious dogmas? Would they gradually build their case by writing editorials accusing him of meddling in politics; would the newspaper publish a few pictures now and then showing him in compromising situations? Would some pastors warn their congregations to keep away from him? Would some people only visit him at night because they are ashamed of what their neighbors might say if they were seen associating with him?

Would those who could not tolerate him strike at him indirectly; would they start to terrorize neighborhoods which had welcomed him? Or would they hire a gang to attack him in an alley? Would he have been more of a nuisance than a peacemaker? Would he look and dress like someone who was poor, and would this have played into the stereotype that people are poor largely through their own fault? Would they ridicule him as the son of an unwed mother? Who would be most likely to notice him, who would be the first to become his friends, and who would cry if he were killed? Would the people most likely to mourn for him have been former drug addicts and prostitutes, or poor people whom he befriended? However unsettling it might be for us to realize its significance, the truth of the matter is that Jesus would not have been born into the social class from which most of us come. We would be very slow to notice him, and very reluctant to travel in his company.

The fact is, Jesus is in the city. He is being born there, he is being raised there, he is learning about people, about himself, about God, and about life there; he is dying there, and he is rising there. He has a life and a presence in all those people, in some more intensely than others, to be sure; but he is in all of them, in their midst. "Whatever you did for one of these least brothers of mine, you did for me." With this he identified with human beings, did he not? Yet who are the least ones, if not the poor, the hungry, the homeless, the children from broken families, those in prison? They may not know about him, but Jesus certainly knows them.

If we cut through any romanticized notions about poverty and prisons, we have to admit that the people with whom Jesus identifies are usually the least attractive. The Son of Man, he said, did not come for the sake of the righteous, but to bring sinners to repentance, and the gospel provides some idea about who these people were. They were spoiled children, as in the story of the prodigal son; they were tax-collectors and prostitutes; they were the derelicts of his day, looking for a meal or for a miracle; they were ordinary, hardworking people, like the first disciples. Many of them probably were rough, uneducated, in need of a bath, and rarely said thanks, like the nine lepers: "Were not ten made clean? Where are the other nine?" Perhaps they did not know how to say thanks. They were people who could easily take advantage of our innocence, or of our guilt over their misfortune. And these were the ones with whom Jesus identified.

True, some of his friends would have been wealthy, but after meeting him their attitude toward wealth, prestige, and power would have been radically altered. Gone from their lives are the country clubs and extra homes and cars. Instead, they are driven with a new-found urgency to refashion society. In Jesus they glimpsed the possibility of the kingdom of God. He taught them that their real neighbors were probably not living next door. Their wealth, their education, their physical well-being, and their positions in society now feel like sums someone has loaned them to invest and to manage wisely.

There Jesus walks, among plain, ordinary men and women who are not especially devout, certainly not known for their virtue, and often disfigured by their poverty, their addictions, their lack of education, their mental disorders, their broken homes. Unlike the rich, they have no cosmetics with which to cover their lives. Who else would still find something loveable about them besides God? There Jesus walks, and breathes, and lives behind a hundred thousand faces. There in the city before us we have the scenes for a contemporary life of Christ, and the only life of Christ which can ever be written is his life in men and women. There are hundreds of thousands of stories to be told. There are as many lives of Christ as there are followers of Christ, for each of our lives is a story about Jesus. The background of those stories is not going to be first-century Palestine but twentieth-century America; it will be as specific as the city or town in which we live. Galilee is every place where the risen Jesus has gone ahead of us.

I hope it does not strike the reader as odd to conclude a book on the baptismal promises this way. We need to think about Christian mission, about the places in which we are likely to imagine Jesus present, since wherever he is, that is where we are going to be drawn. For this the imagination has to be set loose. What shape is the life of Christ taking among men and women of today? If we feel our imaginations drawn but our feet resisting, then perhaps the Spirit is revealing where we have yet to reject sin and face our fears about being with Jesus where he wants to be.

Everything begins with baptism: our introduction into the family of believers, our incorporation into the dying and rising of Jesus, our promise to listen through the whole of our lives to the Word made flesh. That is where the life of Christ in us begins. The story of Jesus in our time can only be the story of his presence and action among us, since what happens to us is happening to him. The only Jesus the world will meet now is the Jesus it finds in us. We do not have to talk about Jesus, however, in the manner of those who badger others about whether they have met the Lord Jesus, or whether they have been saved. There is no need to be pumping him up. Nor should we present him as a make-believe figure, like an imaginary friend.

Yet Jesus is certainly real, and his presence among us can be imagined. People will gather some sense of who he is as they watch us, who do know Jesus. They will form their pictures of him through what we do and

how we speak, through the way we care for and em-
brace one another, through our reverence and compassion, through our practice of faith and the earnestness
of our hope. Among ourselves we must continually
remember and re-tell the story of Jesus, particularly in
the breaking of the bread and the sharing of his cup,
for apart from him we would not be the people we are.
And by telling others about him, we help them to name
the presence which is moving among them. What is he
trying to do? What is he trying to say? What is he
asking of us? Well, to answer that we have to return to
the gospel stories and let Jesus set our imaginations on
fire.

Renewing the Baptis

William Reiser, S.J.

Renewing
the Baptismal Promises

Their Meaning for
Christian Life

Pueblo Publishing Company

New York

Imprimi potest:
Very Rev. Robert E. Manning, S.J.
Provincial, Society of Jesus of New England

Design: Frank Kacmarcik

Scriptural quotations from the New American Bible,
copyright © 1970 by the Confraternity of Christian Doctrine, Washington, D.C., including the revised New
Testament, copyright © 1986. All rights reserved.

Quotations from *The Documents of Vatican II*, Abbott-
Gallagher edition, are reprinted with permission of
America Press, Inc., 106 West 56th Street, New York,
NY 10019, © 1966. All rights reserved.

Quotations from *The Works of Saint Cyril of Jerusalem* are
reprinted with permission of The Catholic University of
America Press, Washington, D.C. © 1970.

Copyright © 1988 Pueblo Publishing Company, Inc.
New York, NY 10001. All rights reserved.

ISBN: 0-916134-89-X

Printed in the United States of America.

Contents